# THE UNOFFICIAL
# ALCATRAZ HANDBOOK

## A COMPLETE GUIDE TO THE MOST OFTEN ASKED QUESTIONS ABOUT "THE ROCK"

FOR RANGER JOHN CANTWELL, WHO OVERSAW ALCATRAZ FOR THE NATIONAL PARK SERVICE FOR OVER THIRTY YEARS. WITHOUT YOU, THIS BOOK WOULD NOT EXIST—KT

TO MY BELOVED, COMPLICATED, AND WONDERFUL CITY BY THE BAY—ON THE UNCEDED HOMELAND OF THE RAMAYTUSH OHLONE—AND TO THE STALWARTS WHO KEEP THE FLICKERING LIGHT OF HER SOUL ALIVE—AO

PENGUIN WORKSHOP
An imprint of Penguin Random House LLC, New York

First published in the United States of America by Penguin Workshop,
an imprint of Penguin Random House LLC, New York, 2024

Text copyright © 2024 by Kristen Tracy
Illustrations copyright © 2024 by Anika Orrock

Visit us online at penguinrandomhouse.com.

Library of Congress Cataloging-in-Publication Data is available.

Manufactured in China

ISBN 9780593661031                                    10 9 8 7 6 5 4 3 2 1 TOPL

Design by Aya Ghanameh

# THE *UNOFFICIAL*
# *ALCATRAZ HANDBOOK*

## A COMPLETE GUIDE TO THE MOST OFTEN ASKED QUESTIONS ABOUT "THE ROCK"

BY KRISTEN TRACY

ILLUSTRATED BY ANIKA ORROCK

PENGUIN WORKSHOP

# CONTENTS

# INTRODUCTION TO ALCATRAZ ISLAND

When I dug into the dirt and my spade struck something, my first thought was, *I've hit a rock*. But as I pulled the object from the dirt, it didn't feel anything like a rock. It wasn't heavy enough, and it had a shape and texture that could only be described as bone-like. It was round and white and fit easily into the palm of my hand—a bone! I think what disturbed me most was where I'd found this bone: I'd unearthed it on Alcatraz Island while removing weeds during a garden restoration project in 2008.

To be exact, I came upon the bone in the prisoners' gardens on the island's windy west side, very near where a set of steep concrete stairs still led down from the prison's recreation yard to a replica guard shack. When it operated as a prison, this was the path the convicts took every day through a metal detector to go to their day jobs on the island. As I held the hollow bone, I wondered if it might belong to a person. It looked like a cut piece of leg bone. How did it end up here? I'd already heard stories from other gardeners about finding things in the dirt, mostly handballs that had sailed over the towering rec-yard wall decades ago. Anything we discovered was considered an artifact and belonged to the island. We had to turn all "finds" over to the head gardener.

A volunteer gardener next to me saw me holding the bone.

"Cool," he said. "You found something."

Was finding a bone *cool*? Maybe.

"How do you think it got here?" I asked.

I watched a lot of true-crime shows. My mind leaped to murder.

"It's a beef bone. They disposed of a lot of kitchen waste in this area," he said. "You never know what you'll find out here. It's a very magical place."

All in all, beef bone included, it turned out to be a good first day volunteering on Alcatraz, even though I'd dressed wrong for hard-core gardening. But soon I would be given a maroon hoodie with a bright purple iris on it that all the volunteers wore. Later I'd receive a gold pin with my name stamped in black. Week after week, I walked along the Embarcadero, a waterfront boulevard in San Francisco, and boarded the staff ferry at Pier 33. I liked sitting on the top level of the boat, watching the island cliff grow closer and closer as we lunged toward it through gray, choppy water. I felt lucky to be traveling to the prison island. Maybe you think I've been curious about Alcatraz my whole life, and that's why I ended up volunteering as a gardener there. It's true that some people are obsessed with everything Alcatraz, but that's not me. Like so many other good things in my life, my time on Alcatraz just sort of happened.

Here's the story: When I moved to San Francisco, I looked for a way to volunteer. I wanted to meet people and find new things to do. I'd grown up sandwiched between small farms in Idaho, so I knew a little bit about gardening. I searched online for projects I could join. The Alcatraz restoration project caught my attention right away because it said I'd get a free weekly boat ride and a special hat. Who could pass up that?

When I finally made it onto the island, so much of the restoration project had already been done. Using old photographs as guides for re-creating the planting beds, gardeners had torn out decades of overgrowth—weeds, blackberries, out-of-control rose bushes—and then repopulated the military officers' gardens and warden's garden, plant by plant and flower by flower. I got there in time to help put back the prisoners' gardens.

Every half hour, large crowds of people exited the boat and pressed up the steep switchback to enter the old shower room in the lower part of the cell house to pick up their headsets and start the audio tour. Lost tourists who'd strayed from the recorded instructions often wandered up to me to ask where to return their headsets. But even after the first two months, I had never taken the prison tour. I had to figure out where to send them. I didn't know much about the remaining buildings on the island or the many layers of history here. I passed the cannon in the sally port (the entry soldiers once had used) every week, but it took me a month before I learned that Alcatraz had previously been a fort. Visit after visit, I discovered new things.

After two years of answering questions from offtrack tourists, I took some training courses and became a tour guide, helping lead visitors through the newly restored gardens. The tours grew so large we needed two guides: a head and a tail. I liked being the tail. I helped open and reset chains and barricades, and I steered curious tourists away from nesting seabirds. Visitors were drawn like magnets to newly hatched seagull chicks, often seeming not to hear the ear-piercing screams of the baby birds' aggressive moms. (Trust me, you do *not* want to tangle with an angry seagull!)

I spent a lot of my time answering questions from visitors who didn't want to interrupt the lead tour guide. I bet I've been asked at least a thousand questions about Alcatraz. Sometimes the same ones pop up over and over. Where was Al Capone's cell? Did anybody ever escape? Why are there so many birds? Could the island be turned into a golf course or a zoo?

I didn't always know the answers. The one firm rule I'd been given was that I wasn't allowed to invent information. So as the questions piled up, I decided to hunt down answers. And although I didn't mean to, I eventually became an unofficial Alcatraz expert.

I ended up spending so much time on the island that I got invited to attend the Alcatraz Alumni Association gatherings, a reunion of former convicts and prison guards that happened every year on the island. Up till then, I'd never met a bank robber. Just like that, I met two: Darwin Coon and Robert Luke. They were sent to Alcatraz because in addition to being bank robbers, they were escape risks. When I met them in 2010, it was hard for me to picture either Darwin or Robert locked up in cellblocks A, B, C, or D, as they strolled past the closed cells, making their way to the annual buffet for lunch.

Hearing the former convicts and guards tell their stories fascinated me. I liked learning about prison life, but I also liked listening to them talk about what they did afterward. I wanted to hear about the lives they had made for themselves after they were released. People clamored for pictures and autographs. But I felt shy around them. When they spoke to big groups about their time in prison (which is what the big groups always wanted to hear about), both bespectacled old men made an effort to share personal details. Their toughened personalities never fully softened, but they always did a good job capturing the crowd's attention. Being around Darwin and Robert made me think about crime and prisons in a different way. I had heard a lot of stories of prisoners serving their time on Alcatraz and leaving the prison system with a new skill or trade and going on to live a crime-free life.

Turns out, I couldn't garden on Alcatraz forever. After a few years, I fell in love with another writer, we moved to the other side of the country, and I became a mom. So I gave up my work as a gardener and a tour guide. Whenever anybody finds out I used to be a volunteer gardener on Alcatraz, they have lots of questions. And I try really hard to answer every single one.

This book includes answers to the twenty most often asked questions I remember getting from visitors on the island.

But the number one question people ask on Alcatraz is: Where are the bathrooms? Just so you know, there are two public bathrooms, and I've included a handy map that shows their exact locations. You'll notice that in addition to the questions, this book includes sections called "You Can Still See It Today." I spent so many Sunday mornings giving tours and pointing out all the historic details that I want to make sure everybody can see them here, too, and notice all the special little layers of history tucked away or sometimes hidden in plain sight.

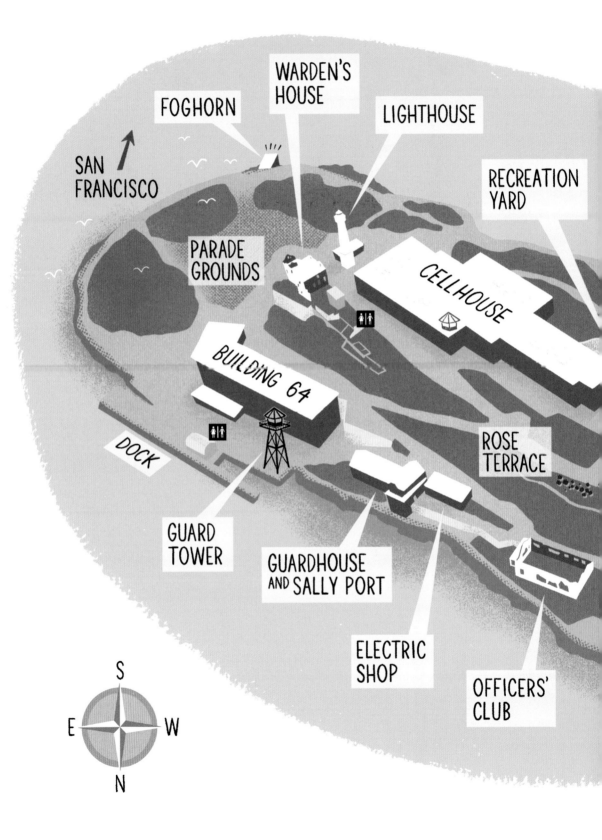

# ALCATRAZ
## ISLAND

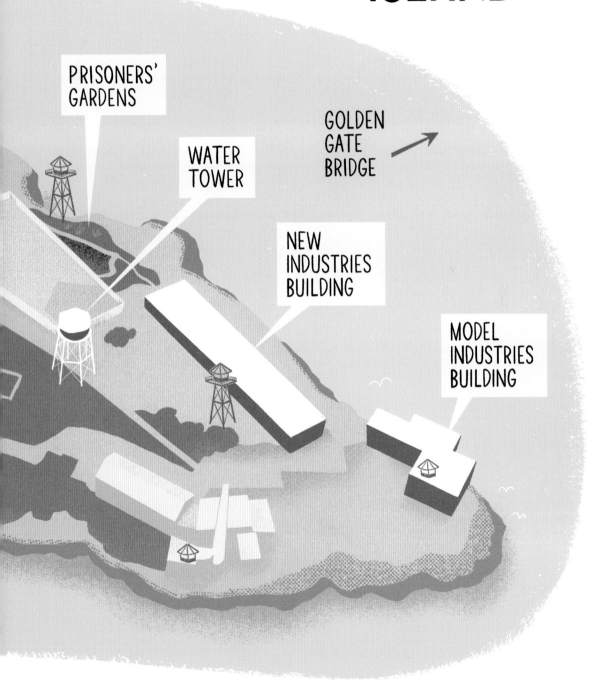

PRISONERS' GARDENS

WATER TOWER

GOLDEN GATE BRIDGE

NEW INDUSTRIES BUILDING

MODEL INDUSTRIES BUILDING

# CHAPTER 1
# HOW DID ALCATRAZ GET ITS NAME?

The story of how Alcatraz got its name comes with a few twists. Historically speaking, Alcatraz hasn't always been important. In fact, it wasn't even noticed. When European explorers sailed along the coast of California, claiming territory for the Spanish and later the British crowns, they failed to see San Francisco Bay and sailed right past it for two hundred years. Either fog obscured it, or the placement of Alcatraz right in the center of the Golden Gate (the strait that connects San Francisco Bay to the Pacific Ocean) gave the illusion that it was solid coastline. It wasn't until 1769 that a small group of Spanish soldiers on a land-exploration journey under the command of Gaspar de Portolá overshot their real destination, Monterey Bay, and stumbled across the San Francisco Bay on foot.

The Spanish entered San Francisco Bay by ship for the first time in 1775. They mapped and named all the larger islands. Charts from this time appear to label the island currently called Yerba Buena as the Isla de los Alcatraces. For fifty years, Spanish maps labeled Yerba Buena Island *Alcatraces*, and the island we now know as Alcatraz remained unlabeled. Alcatraz didn't get its current name until 1827, when British officer Captain Frederick Beechey put the name *Alcatraces* next to present-day Alcatraz Island and added the label *Yerba Buena* next to present-day Yerba Buena Island. A lot of people refer to Alcatraz as the "Island of Pelicans," but that might not be totally accurate.

The Spanish word for a "seabird" is *alcatraz*, and the Spanish word for "seabirds" is *alcatraces*. So the Isla de los Alcatraces could refer to pelicans, cormorants, gannets, or maybe all of these. Here are just a few of the names that were once used for the island: Alcatras, Alcatrose, Alcatrazas, Alcatrazos, Alcatruces, Alcatrus, and Alcatraz.

But was anyone on the island before Europeans arrived? Located 1.25 miles off the coast of the city of San Francisco, it's likely either the Muwekma Ohlone or the Coast Miwok canoed to the island. There's no proof that First Nations settled or lived on the island in any permanent way. Some people think that both the Ohlone and Miwok visited the island to forage for seabird eggs. Since First Nations pass down their traditions and histories orally, and much of their cultures were wiped out after Europeans arrived, there's no clear answer for how, or if, the Ohlone or Miwok used Alcatraz.

The earliest days of Alcatraz are a mystery. What we do know is that it was a perfect sanctuary for nesting seabirds, and we're pretty sure it was covered in white bird poop. Exactly how the Muwekma Ohlone or Coast Miwok used the rock island for three thousand years is something we'll just continue to wonder about.

# YOU CAN STILL SEE IT TODAY

A common nickname for this island is "The Rock." If you walk along the main road that leads to the top of the island and the prison cell house, you'll pass tall rock cliffs that look like a giant, dark, hard wall. This is the actual sandstone that the island of Alcatraz is made out of. Reach out and drag your hand along it; you're touching The Rock.

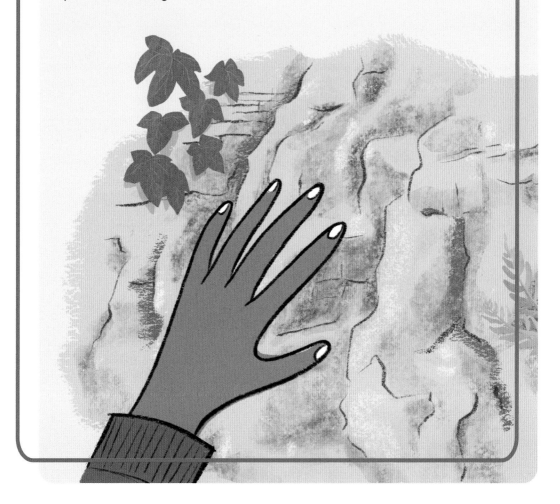

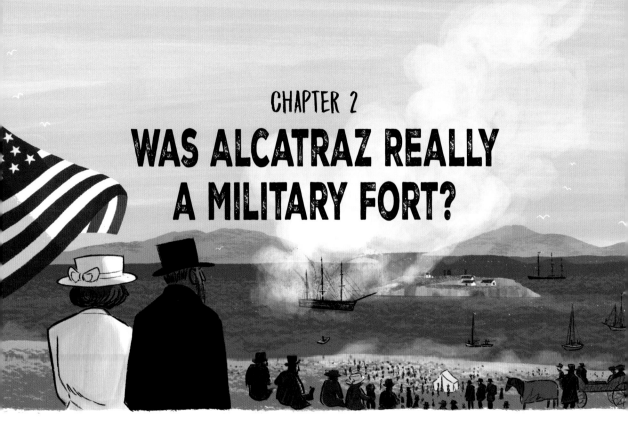

# CHAPTER 2
# WAS ALCATRAZ REALLY A MILITARY FORT?

T he reason Alcatraz is preserved today isn't because of its history as a maximum-security prison that incarcerated some of America's most famous gangsters; it's because for nearly ninety years, the US Army occupied and reshaped the rock island, then used it as a fort. Alcatraz Island became government property in 1848, after the Mexican-American War ended. At the same time the US government was deciding what to do with Alcatraz, the Gold Rush started, and San Francisco and its bay became something worth protecting. The initial plan was to have three forts on three different pieces of land that created a nearly impenetrable triangle: one fort on either side of the narrowest point of the Golden Gate and Fort Alcatraz in the middle. They built Fort Point on the south side of the strait and built Fort Alcatraz in the middle, but the government was never able to negotiate a price for the land on the northern side of the strait, so the third fort never got built.

Building a fort on Alcatraz was nearly impossible. It was a solid rock, lacking any natural water or soil. Wind battered the island constantly, large numbers of seabirds inhabited it, a thick fog enveloped it, strong currents pressed around it, and there was only one small spot to dock a ship. Not only was it difficult to get building materials to the island, but workers would often abandon their jobs to go mine for gold in other parts of California. Using an explosive mixture called black powder, the US Army Corps of Engineers began blasting away portions of the rock to make the ground level.

The island needed to be equipped with cannons to defend the bay, a lighthouse to help guide marine traffic, roads, water cisterns (underground containers to store water), latrines, buildings, fortified walls, and the ever-important fort itself: a three-story barracks (building used to house soldiers), located on top of the island, called the Citadel. This was also where many of the soldiers slept. The military protected this building with a dry moat and two drawbridges. In 1854, the island received its first armament of eleven cannons. That same year, the lighthouse was lit for the first time, using a special lens shipped from France that could illuminate the light of a whale-oil flame for nineteen nautical miles. Construction of buildings was a near-constant activity carried out under very harsh conditions. In 1857, the first fatalities were recorded on Alcatraz. Two men, Daniel Pewter and Jacob Unger, were buried under a rockslide while excavating along the main roadway. A mule was also killed in the slide.

Fort Alcatraz was nearing completion just as the country lurched toward the Civil War. Alcatraz operated as a Union stronghold, protecting the harbor against people who lived in San Francisco and sided with the Confederacy. At the start of the war, the man overseeing Alcatraz, Kentucky-born Colonel Albert Sidney Johnston, moved ten thousand muskets and 150,000 rounds of ammunition to the island to keep it out of Confederate hands.

As the war rolled on, fears grew that Confederate warships skulked in San Francisco Bay. In 1863, the military caught wind of a ship called the *J. M. Chapman*, full of secessionists, hoping to blockade the bay. They believed that Confederate forces could take the city. The navy boarded the ship, found ammunition and cannons, and discovered that one of the men had a letter signed by Jefferson Davis, president of the Confederate States of America, granting him a spot in the Confederate Navy. All of these men were found guilty of treason and sentenced to prison time on Alcatraz.

When the Civil War ended, so did the era of Alcatraz's importance as a harbor defense post. Advances in weaponry meant that instead of using smoothbore cannons that lobbed loosely aimed objects short distances, ships now fired rifled cannons. These new cannons with spiraled barrels could precisely aim and shoot from tremendous distances, easily crumbling brick walls. So before it was finished being built, Alcatraz was pretty much useless as a fort. Its walls were no longer a great defense.

From 1847 to 1907, Alcatraz Island continued to operate as a fort but fired her own cannons only two times at ships. First, on October 1, 1863, unable to identify the flag on an incoming ship's mast, Fort Alcatraz fired at the British navy ship the *HMS Sutlej*, lobbing a four-hundred-pound cannonball in front of her, stopping her in her tracks. And second, on the United States' one-hundred-year anniversary, when San Francisco planned a mock July 3, 1776, battle, staged just for show. The navy planned to destroy an old schooner stocked with explosives using three of its warships. The battle began at 11:30 a.m. and lasted a long time.

After firing more than a hundred rounds, the target ship remained perfectly fine, and an officer had to row out and light the fuse to unleash the explosive fury the public had been waiting for.

Her fort days behind her, on March 21, 1907, Alcatraz was officially designated the Pacific Branch, US Military Prison by the War Department, serving the army for all states and territory west of the Rocky Mountains.

## YOU CAN STILL SEE IT TODAY

As you enter the sally port, look up and you'll see "Alcatraces Island 1857" etched in stone. This carving was revealed in 2015 during construction to strengthen the building. In the adjoining room, you'll find a grate-covered trapdoor that leads to a prison below. In the room across the way, you'll see a 24-pounder Howitzer cannon. Over the years, many different types of cannons and cannonballs were used on Alcatraz, as well as multiple furnaces to heat the cannonballs, creating hot shots. The hope was the heated cannonballs would strike and burn enemy wooden ships. Old photographs reveal that the cannonballs were often stored in decorative ways across the island.

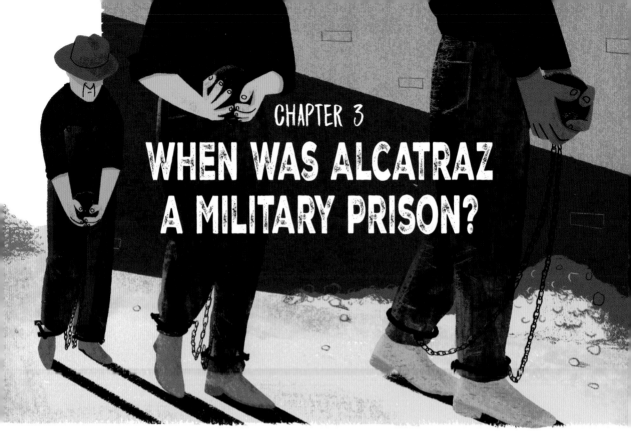

# CHAPTER 3
# WHEN WAS ALCATRAZ A MILITARY PRISON?

In 1859, at the same time Alcatraz began operating as a fort, the first prisoners were deposited on the island. Out of the eighty-six men who arrived as part of an artillery regiment, eleven were shackled in the basement of the guardhouse for crimes unknown. The military quickly realized that the strong currents and cold waters surrounding Alcatraz made helpful deterrents for escape, and from this point on, the number of prisoners on Alcatraz would continue to climb.

Military prisoners were sentenced to Alcatraz for a variety of crimes: desertion (abandonment of military duties with intent not to come back), stealing, murder, and more. These prisoners often endured brutal conditions, such as carrying a twelve-pound metal chain and ball, even when assigned to work details or while chained to walls. Prisoners were branded on their hips with a *D* (deserter) or *T* (thief) until the 1870s, when they received these labels as tattoos.

As the prisoner population increased, it began to include soldiers who were guilty of other crimes. Dozens of men were arrested in California for openly celebrating Lincoln's assassination. Thirty-nine of them were sentenced to Alcatraz. Members of religious groups such as the Quakers, Hutterites, and Mennonites claiming conscientious-objector status (those who refuse to perform military service) during World War 1 were sentenced there. Many members of First Nations who wanted to keep their religions, traditions, and languages were labeled "hostiles" and brought to Alcatraz to be punished. The army sent their own scouts who had been convicted of mutiny to Alcatraz, along with Modoc Indians from the Modoc War in northeast California (famously among them, Sloluck and Barncho) and some of Geronimo's lieutenants. In 1895, Chief Lomahongewma and eighteen other Hopi men resisted sending their children from the reservation to public schools (which were often far from their homes and full of disease), and they were sent to Alcatraz and held there for nearly a year.

In 1906, while San Francisco smoldered following a deadly earthquake, national guardsmen loaded 176 ruffians, muggers, thieves, drunken partiers, and other criminals from San Francisco's badly damaged Broadway Jail, Hall of Justice Jail, and Ingleside Jails onto a boat bound for San Quentin prison, north of the city. But the warden there turned them away. So the men were delivered to Alcatraz, which had only received minimal damage from the quake, just a few cracked chimneys and pipes. As the inmate population continued to grow, the government decided to knock down the old Citadel and build a new cell house where it had stood. From 1909 to 1911, prisoners on Alcatraz built the new US Disciplinary Barracks for the US Army, which was designed to hold six hundred prisoners.

At the time, it was the largest steel-enforced concrete structure in the world. The new prison facility opened on February 6, 1912, and operated until 1933. Some of the most interesting prison escapes occurred during the time it was the US Disciplinary Barracks, including four men who stole a butter vat and tried to row it ashore, but wind and currents sent them back to the island. A very similar event occurred the following year involving three escapees and a dough-kneading trough—a shallow, rectangular basin that they used like a small canoe. Anything a prisoner found that could float, he'd try to sail to freedom, including a ladder that almost took two men all the way out to sea. A man named Jack Allen attempted the final escape during the military-prison era by taking off all his clothes, greasing his body, and leaping into the chilly water. Jack was never seen again.

Soaring upkeep costs led the US military to turn over control of the prison island to the Bureau of Prisons in 1933. The US Department of Justice had been looking for an isolated place to build a new, inescapable, maximum-security prison capable of housing the worst of the worst.

## YOU CAN STILL SEE IT TODAY

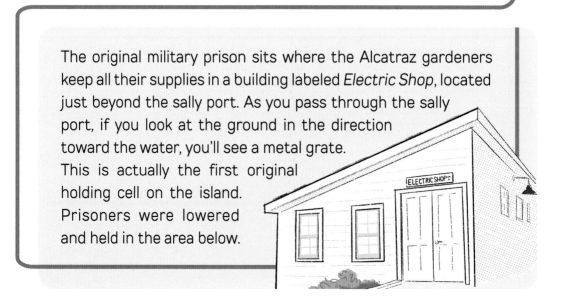

The original military prison sits where the Alcatraz gardeners keep all their supplies in a building labeled *Electric Shop*, located just beyond the sally port. As you pass through the sally port, if you look at the ground in the direction toward the water, you'll see a metal grate. This is actually the first original holding cell on the island. Prisoners were lowered and held in the area below.

ELECTRIC SHOP

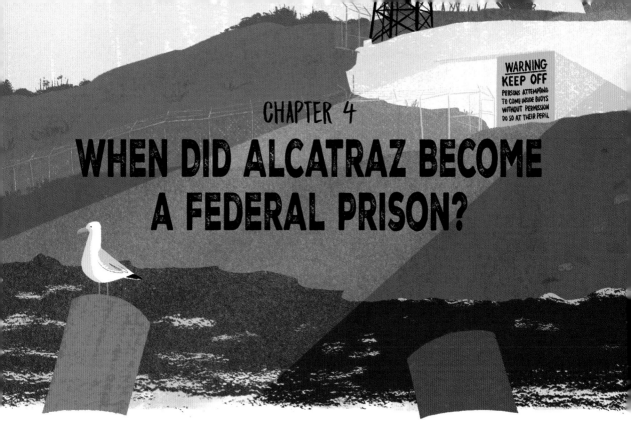

# CHAPTER 4
# WHEN DID ALCATRAZ BECOME A FEDERAL PRISON?

On October 12, 1933, the secretary of war signed a lease for the island of Alcatraz with the Bureau of Prisons, and on June 20, 1934, the army turned Alcatraz over to Warden James Johnston. The Rock's eighty-seven years of military history finally came to an end. While the military prisoners didn't need to be held in a maximum-security facility, the incoming group of America's worst gangsters, who the FBI and its director, J. Edgar Hoover, hoped to lock up there, certainly did.

Alcatraz would undergo many adjustments before it could become the "super" prison that J. Edgar dreamed it to be. All the window sashes and 336 of the cell fronts were torn out and replaced with tool-resistant steel bars. Locks on the cell doors in B, C, and D blocks were replaced with locking devices operated by control boxes supplied by Stewart Iron Works in Cincinnati.

Three new guard towers were built (in addition to the one that already existed), and a fifth emergency tower was installed on the island's northeast side. They were to be manned around the clock, giving armed officers a bird's-eye view of every inch of the island. Prisoners would always be "under the gun."

Large signs were posted warning watercraft to keep at least two hundred yards away or risk being shot at. Additionally, orange buoys ringed the island at three hundred yards, creating what was called a "dead line." Anybody who entered this area risked being fired upon. East and west gun galleries—narrow, elevated walkways where armed guards could oversee prisoners—were built inside the prison cell house, which was where prisoners slept and lived. The gun galleries would be the only two places within the prison where guards were armed with guns. Metal detectors were added outside the prison cafeteria and the entrances to the prison workshops. Thousands of feet of barbed wire were spread across the island to create a clear barrier between the prisoners and the families of the guards who'd be living on the island. The wire was also strung to prevent easy access to the island's cliffs and the buildings closest to the sea. Numerous tear gas canisters were fitted in columns in the cafeteria and also above the main gate between the cell house and the administrative offices. Switches to release them were located nearby, but they were never used.

The people living in San Francisco were deeply upset that a maximum-security prison was going to be established in their bay. Even the chief of police in San Francisco, William J. Quinn, thought it was a bad idea. He argued that unlike when it held military prisoners for short sentences, imprisoning criminals on the island with much longer sentences would increase their incentive to escape. It would be a source of tension throughout the prison's entire existence. The *San Francisco*

*Chronicle* printed many editorials deeply opposed to the prison. One pointed out that, over the years, at least twenty-three military prisoners had managed to escape from the island, some by stealing a boat and some by swimming to shore.

On August 1, 1934, US Attorney General Homer Stille Cummings and Federal Bureau of Prisons Director Sanford Bates officially activated Alcatraz as a federal penitentiary, a prison for those who have committed serious crimes.

## YOU CAN STILL SEE IT TODAY

The cell house remains the most intact building on the island. All four cellblocks, A, B, C and D; prison dining hall; warden's office; clerk's office; visiting area; and the recreation yard are open to the public. The east and west gun galleries, and what remains of the catwalk (elevated walkway) surrounding the rec yard look a lot like they did when the prison closed in 1963. And the flat bars in A-Block from the military prison years are different from the maximum-security, tool-proof steel bars in cellblocks B, C, and D.

# CHAPTER 5
# WHAT KIND OF CRIMINALS ENDED UP ON ALCATRAZ?

The goal of Alcatraz prison, from the beginning, was to house the worst types of criminals. It operated as a prison for other federal prisons. Usually, convicts sent to Alcatraz were being punished for offenses they had committed in other prisons, often escape attempts. After serving time on the island, they were then sent to finish their sentences in another prison. It was rare for an inmate to be released directly into society from Alcatraz. Some inmates who wanted a chance at parole didn't bother applying for it until after they were transferred because they knew nearly all parole requests made from Alcatraz were denied.

At the time, there was a lot of pressure on the government to build a prison like Alcatraz. During the 1920s and 1930s, some criminals were actually becoming famous for the crimes they had committed: Bonnie and Clyde, Machine Gun

Kelly, John Dillinger, Al Capone, and Pretty Boy Floyd, just to name a few. A lot of these outlaws liked to rob things: trains, banks, stores, and post offices. In 1932, the American Bankers Association recorded 631 bank robberies. Then a wave of kidnappings started. The US government began changing laws to make acts such as robbing a bank or post office, or kidnapping a person and taking them across state lines, into federal crimes. That meant they were punishable at the national level, rather than by states. In 1932, Lester Gillis, known as Baby Face Nelson, broke out of a state prison in Joliet, Illinois. In 1933, famed bank robber Harvey Bailey busted out of the Kansas State Penitentiary with four other prisoners. John Dillinger, on parole, orchestrated the escape of ten prisoners from the Indiana State Prison in Michigan City. That same year, Dillinger shot and killed a sheriff while escaping from a jail in Lima, Ohio. But escape wasn't the only problem with America's prisons. There was a lot of corruption, too, where inmates could pay for better treatment and "favors."

In the 1920s, the FBI (simply the "Bureau of Investigation" at that time) sent undercover agents to prisons around the country to see how bad the corruption had gotten. They found that influential inmates could pay for almost anything, including preferred jobs, shared cells with friends, and transfers to different prisons. Al Capone made headlines for the special treatment he got in prisons in both Philadelphia and Atlanta: feather pillows, a typewriter, shaving gear, a full set of encyclopedias, extra underwear, ice cream, colorful rugs, tennis shoes, a tennis racket with a hollowed-out handle stuffed with cash, and more.

The FBI didn't want to send the worst offenders to a prison where they could buy favors and preferable treatment. They wanted to punish them by confining them in a place where a person only had four rights: food, shelter, clothing, and medical care. Everything else was a privilege that had to be earned. No newspapers.

No radio. No commissary (a prison store). No visitors were allowed for the first three months. After that, an Alcatraz prisoner could receive only one visit a month (from a relative), conducted through bulletproof glass while speaking on a telephone.

Alcatraz inmates were allowed one outgoing letter a week and could receive up to seven incoming letters. In the beginning, Warden James Johnston was worried about invisible ink being used to send secret messages to the prisoners, so he ordered all letters to be retyped. The men never even got to see their family members' own handwriting! Incoming mail was so tightly controlled that it could only come from a list of five members of the prisoner's immediate family. Around 1940, however, these rules began to loosen.

## YOU CAN STILL SEE IT TODAY

The typical cell in Alcatraz measures five feet by nine feet with a seven-foot-high ceiling. Isolation was a big part of the Alcatraz experience.

A visitor would meet the inmate at the top of the cell house, opposite the cafeteria. You can still see the bulletproof glass and the phone prisoners used to talk to their family members. Remember, prisoners only got one visitor a month, and that was only if a family member could make it all the way to Alcatraz Island.

# CHAPTER 6
# WHAT BUILDINGS WERE BUILT ON THE ISLAND?

Alcatraz Island didn't just hold a maximum-security prison; the island held a small city.

The building closest to the dock is Building 64. During the military era, it served as a "bombproof" army barracks. To house more soldiers, the military turned it into a three-story barracks in 1905. When it became a federal prison, the building was converted into twenty-six apartments to house the families of correctional officers. The renovations left an oddly made structure with blocked-off fireplaces and staircases, and hallways that didn't lead anywhere. Building 64 also contained a post office. During its military days, the large, square windows that surrounded it acted as cannon ports. Today, it's the only remaining residential structure on the island.

Across the island, there were six guard towers: dock tower, power plant roof, model industries roof, hill tower, road tower, and cell house roof. And at the island's flattened peak sat the prison cell house. In addition to cellblocks A, B, C, and D, the cell house contained a prison library, hospital, warden's office, administrative office, correctional officers' lounge, control center, armory (weapons storage), visitors' room, cafeteria, kitchen, barbershop, shower room, band room, print shop, refrigeration room, chaplain's office, auditorium/chapel, and the clothing-issue room. There was a recreation yard for the prisoners, where many spent time playing bridge or softball.

Near the top of the island, close to the cell house, was the warden's house, a three-story, fifteen-room mansion. The island also had a lighthouse and the lighthouse keeper's home, which burned down in 1970, along with several other historic buildings, including the doctor's home. The island had two foghorn buildings on opposite ends of the island, which the families living on the island named Bellowing Bull and Moaning Cow. At the base of the island was the post exchange, which became the officers' club during the prison era (and was also destroyed in the 1970 fire). It contained two bowling alleys, a soda fountain, and space to watch movies and put on plays. The parade grounds were used as a playground for the children of Alcatraz. One building the island lacked was a school. Children had to travel by boat to the mainland for that. They were issued special tags that they wore around their necks that identified them as residents of Alcatraz. Two rules on the island that children had to follow were: no pets and no toy guns. Also, residents weren't allowed to throw away razors, tools, clothing, or bottles with their trash. Those types of things were thrown directly into the bay.

The island had quite a bit of residential housing on the parade grounds, including apartment buildings for families and also single officers. The island also had a powerhouse, a water tower, a morgue, a quartermaster warehouse

(warehouse space for items ranging from pipes to furniture), a toolshed, and a greenhouse in the rose garden. And of course there was a wharf, which had an X-ray machine that inspected all incoming supplies for contraband (things that had been brought onto the island illegally). Prisoners worked in the industries area, which contained two buildings: the new industries and the model industries buildings.

For the families to live there safely, the prisoners needed to be closely guarded.

Inmates celled alone, and for the first years of operation, prisoners weren't allowed to talk except in whispers at mealtimes and in the rec yard on weekends. Here's how a typical day began for an inmate:

6:30 a.m.: the morning gong. The inmate made his bed and ordered his things, wiping everything down.

6:50 a.m.: the second morning gong. By the cell door, he stood, facing the guard and staying that way until the guard's whistle. They made their count of prisoners, and if correct, the cells unlocked.

6:55 a.m.: first whistle. The prisoner stepped out of his cell and turned toward the cafeteria. Second whistle: He joined a single-file line.

7:00 a.m.: third whistle. Designated cellblocks walked to the cafeteria, following a precise order. Each prisoner followed that order and was given twenty minutes to eat. He could take all he wanted, but he had to eat all the food he took. When finished, he arranged the utensils as they were supposed to be and waited with his hands at his sides. The guards would come and inspect his tray. If he had a job, he'd move out the rear door to the rec yard in a very specific order.

There were counts to enter and counts during the day. Twelve official counts were made every twenty-four hours; one head count every two hours. Two showers a week, unless a prisoner worked in the cafeteria; then, he showered every day.

# YOU CAN STILL SEE IT TODAY

The laundry facilities where Al Capone and many other prisoners worked doing laundry for officers stationed at military bases in the San Francisco area have been restored. Today, the laundry rooms occasionally feature art exhibits.

# CHAPTER 7
# WHAT TYPES OF JOBS DID THE PRISONERS HAVE?

**W**ork was a privilege on the island, but most prisoners liked having jobs because they broke up the boredom and allowed them to earn extra money. According to inmates, the best place to work was the cafeteria. Having access to extra food meant that it could be given to other convicts for favors. And it meant daily showers. Many convicts also enjoyed working in the gardens because it gave them freedom. A few of the inmate gardeners would take flowers back to their cells and keep them in their drinking cups.

Some of the more interesting jobs included working in the new industries building to manufacture cargo nets and also repair large buoys that secured submarine nets used to protect San Francisco Bay from Japanese submarines during World War II. But other jobs were seen as difficult, like garbage assignment. Prison labor was used for everything from plumbing to electric work to painting.

Men on the island did laundry for the military, so there were many, many jobs in that department.

Quite a few jobs either taught or required specialized skills. Jim Quillen worked as an X-ray technician in the hospital, and he used the skills he learned to land a job when he got out. Elliott Michener built a greenhouse on Alcatraz in which he grew flowers for the warden's wife. Alvin Karpis worked as a baker, a skill he learned before he became "Public Enemy Number One." Clarence Anglin worked as an Alcatraz barber. Some men worked at the docks unloading goods.

The only time convicts didn't go to work were on days of thick fog. This rule was implemented after Theodore "Ted" Cole and Ralph Roe, two convicted bank robbers, escaped the island after sneaking away from their jobs in the model industries building on December 16, 1937. Ted worked as a janitor in the blacksmith shop, and Ralph worked in the mat shop, turning used tires into mats for the navy. The fog was so thick that winter morning that gun-tower guards didn't have enough visibility, and convicts were sent back to their cells.

But when the fog began to lift, inmates were allowed to return to their jobs. On Alcatraz, inmates were counted at their jobs every thirty minutes. At 1:00 p.m., Ted and Ralph were exactly where they were supposed to be. At 1:30 p.m., they'd vanished. For months, they'd been sawing out bars in a window. The fog gave them the cover they needed to try to swim to shore. They climbed out the window—now free of its bars—and used a wrench to break open a fence, then ran to the water. Other inmates saw them go under the choppy waves and never come back up. There were fourteen escape attempts on Alcatraz; eleven occurred while convicts were working at their prison jobs.

Walking north along the Embarcadero to Fisherman's Wharf in San Francisco, look for blue telescopes along the water's edge. If you aim a telescope at the island, you'll be able to see Alcatraz. When it was a prison, people used to look into the telescopes as prisoners were released down the stairs from the rec yard to go to work in the new industries building. You can focus the telescope on the stairs they walked down.

In photographs of prisoners descending those stairs, they are seen looking down, hiding their faces. They did this because they didn't like people looking at them from across the bay.

# CHAPTER 8

# WHO WERE THE MOST FAMOUS PRISONERS ON ALCATRAZ?

A lot of well-known criminals have been housed on Alcatraz. Here are some of the most famous.

## Alphonse "Al" Capone, AKA "Scarface"

See Chapter Nine.

## George "Machine Gun" Kelly Barnes

George Kelly Barnes was born in 1897 in Chicago. He attended college in 1917 at the University of Mississippi, where he studied engineering and agriculture and met his first wife, Geneva. The following year, George dropped out of school and started a family. George had a difficult time finding a job and began bootlegging (making, selling, or illegally supplying alcohol). After an arrest in 1923, he changed his name to protect his family's reputation—and also to evade law enforcement. He headed west, and became George R. Kelly.

George got caught and sent to prison a few more times. Then he had the bad luck of meeting his second wife, Kathryn Thorne. She was a very experienced criminal who bought him a Tommy submachine gun and taught him how to use it by shooting walnuts off a fence. She created the name "Machine Gun Kelly" for him. George's bank robberies eventually led to the kidnapping of Oklahoma oil tycoon Charles F. Urschel.

Not wanting to endanger his life, the Urschel family paid the full ransom, $200,000. George and Kathryn ran from the law, burying their ransom money in thermoses, as they fled to Tennessee. They were eventually captured, and George got a life sentence. The case became famous for many reasons. The steep ransom, $200,000, was the largest amount ever demanded at that time. And it was the first American trial to allow cameras in the courtroom.

George died in Leavenworth prison of a heart attack on his fifty-ninth birthday after spending twenty-one years behind bars. Seventeen of those were on Alcatraz, where he was prisoner number 117. Albert Bates, an accomplice in Charles's kidnapping and a longtime bank-robbing partner of George's, was also sentenced to Alcatraz, as prisoner number 137, where he died on the island in 1948.

George was a model prisoner while on Alcatraz, where he earned a new nickname, "Popgun Kelly" (a popgun is a type of toy gun), because he wasn't fierce at all.

## Harvey Bailey

Harvey Bailey was born on August 23, 1887, in Jane Lew, West Virginia. Harvey was one of the most successful bank robbers in America. He was an escape artist, too. While serving a fifty-year sentence in the Kansas State Penitentiary in 1933, Harvey, along with ten other inmates, broke out in spectacular fashion, taking the prison warden hostage and using him as a human shield. Once free, he continued to rob banks. He probably would have kept at it if not for his decision to visit Machine Gun Kelly's Texas ranch hideout to return a machine gun and also collect some money that was owed to him. While Harvey slept, the FBI showed up to search the property because they suspected it might be connected to the Charles Urschel kidnapping.

FBI agents were stunned at the good luck of stumbling upon America's most-wanted bank robber and promptly arrested him. Less than a month later, Harvey managed to escape from his Texas jail cell. But when he'd been recaptured with over $700 of the Charles Urschel ransom money in his pocket, Harvey was tried and convicted as an accomplice for a kidnapping that he had nothing to do with. He was sent to Leavenworth in 1933, but then in 1934, he was transferred to Alcatraz, where he was given the number 139. He served twelve years on Alcatraz before being sent back to Leavenworth.

Harvey was released from prison in 1964 when he was seventy-six years old. He worked as a cabinetmaker until his death at age ninety-one.

## Roy Gardner

Roy Gardner was born on January 5, 1884, in Trenton, Missouri. Roy liked excitement. He joined the army, became a gunrunner in Mexico, a boxer in the United States, and eventually, a jewel thief. Sent to San Quentin for a jewelry store robbery, he surprisingly was released early after helping save the life of a guard during a prison riot.

Once free, Roy became a welder. He got married and had a daughter. But on a business trip to Mexico, he gambled away all his money and decided to rob $80,000 from a mail train. Roy found that he loved robbing trains. On the West Coast, he was as famous as Jesse James. Roy was eventually captured while burying his stolen money and sentenced to twenty-five years on McNeil Island, off the coast of Washington state. While being transported to the prison by train, Roy outwitted the lawmen guarding him, handcuffed them together, and escaped.

He became known as the "Smiling Bandit" and was captured again while playing cards in a pool hall but managed to escape—again while being transported! This triggered the largest manhunt on the Pacific coast in US history. Roy was soon captured robbing another train. He was eventually sent to Alcatraz in 1934. While there, he began writing the story of his life, *Hellcatraz*, which would be the first account of life inside those secretive prison walls. Since he'd never injured anyone during the commission of his crimes, Roy's appeal for clemency was approved in 1938.

Out of prison, Roy lost all his money in Hollywood, trying to turn his life story into a movie. On December 10, 1940, Roy died in a hotel room in San Francisco. He left a note on the outside of his door that read: "Do not open this door. Poison gas. Call police." He was only fifty-six years old.

## Alvin "Creepy" Karpis

Throughout its history, the FBI has only labeled four criminals as "Public Enemy Number One," a name assigned during the Depression to the nation's most dangerous and most-wanted criminals: John Dillinger, Pretty Boy Floyd, Baby Face Nelson, and Alvin Karpis. Alvin is the only outlaw on this list to be captured alive.

Francis Albin Karpowicz, the son of Lithuanian immigrants, was born in

Montreal, Canada, on August 10, 1907. When he was eight years old, his family moved to Topeka, Kansas, and a teacher changed his name to Alvin Karpis because it was easier to pronounce. Most accounts, including his own, say that Alvin began committing crimes at age ten, when he stole his first gun. While serving time at the Kansas State Penitentiary, Alvin met Fred Barker of the "Bloody Barkers" and began a friendship that turned into a criminal partnership. They would be known as the Karpis-Barker Gang, which included Fred's criminal brothers: Herman, Lloyd, and Arthur (known as Doc).

Alvin had a knack for avoiding capture. His file lists fifteen bank robberies, four murders, three jailbreaks, and two kidnappings—William Hamm, president of Hamm Brewing Company, for a $100,000 ransom and Edward Bremer, president of Commercial State Bank, for a $200,000 ransom (the bills from the second kidnapping were marked and therefore much harder to spend). J. Edgar Hoover wanted to personally capture him in front of a lot of cameras. Alvin made a wild escape in a shootout in Atlantic City that enraged J. Edgar. It didn't help that both kidnapping victims were friends of then-president Franklin Delano Roosevelt.

After he robbed two mail trains in Ohio, the FBI eventually caught up with Alvin in New Orleans. When he exited the house where he'd been staying, agents pounced. They held him at gunpoint and waited for J. Edgar Hoover to appear so he could be photographed capturing Alvin. But when J. Edgar arrived and asked for handcuffs, not a single officer had a pair. They'd planned to shoot up the place, not make an arrest. Alvin was secured using one of the agent's neckties.

Alvin pled guilty to the Hamm kidnapping and received a life sentence.

Alvin Karpis spent more time on Alcatraz than any other inmate, a total of twenty-six years, from 1936 to 1962. Once back in Canada, Alvin got to work writing his memoir, *On the Rock*, where he talks openly about his time in prison and his fellow inmates. Alvin moved to Spain in 1973 and died six years later at the age of seventy-two.

## Robert "Birdman" Stroud

Robert Franklin Stroud, the Birdman of Alcatraz, was born in 1890 in Seattle, Washington. Robert had an abusive childhood and ran away from home at thirteen and ended up in Alaska. He became good friends with a woman named Kate Dulaney, who got into a violent argument with a local bartender. Robert took Kate's pistol and shot the bartender to death. After returning the gun to Kate, Robert surrendered himself to authorities. He was eighteen years old.

Robert never had a trial. In 1909, he pled guilty to manslaughter, taking a plea deal to dodge a murder charge and avoid the death penalty. While in Leavenworth, a much bigger, much newer, and more secure prison, Robert focused on his education, taking long-distance courses in astronomy, mathematics, and structural engineering.

A few years into his prison sentence, using a shiv he always carried with him, Robert stabbed a prison guard, killing him instantly in front of over a thousand witnesses.

For this murder, Robert was sentenced to die by hanging. But Robert's mother convinced the president of the United States, Woodrow Wilson, to commute Robert's death sentence to life in prison, with the condition that he would remain in solitary confinement. Robert would go on to spend fifty-four years in prison. Over forty of those were in solitary confinement (meaning that he was kept in a separate cell, away from other prisoners).

The reason Robert is known as the "Birdman of Alcatraz" is a bit confusing. He didn't actually work with birds while on Alcatraz.

His interest in birds began in 1920 when he was still in Leavenworth prison. One day in the prison yard, Robert came across a fallen nest with baby sparrows in it. He took it back to his cell and nursed them back to health. He began keeping more and more birds. He turned his educational focus to ornithology, the study of birds. He loved canaries, and at one time, Robert had over three hundred birds, which prison staff allowed him to keep in the cell next to his own. Robert became such an expert in birds and their diseases that he wrote and published two books, *Diseases of Canaries* (1933) and *Stroud's Digest on the Diseases of Birds* (1943). To learn as much as he could about the birds, after they died, Robert dissected them using his fingernails.

The Leavenworth prison staff grew tired of Robert and his birds, but he became a celebrity. Thomas E. Gaddis wrote a popular book about Robert that was made into a movie starring Burt Lancaster, *Birdman of Alcatraz*. People assume to this day that Robert kept birds at Alcatraz, but he was never allowed to have birds on the island. All the work he did with canaries was done in Leavenworth. Robert was separated from his birds and taken to Alcatraz against his wishes in 1942. While on Alcatraz, Robert was a problematic inmate, disliked by both guards and other prisoners. He was seen as unstable and remained in solitary confinement in D-Block and in a large cell in the hospital wing.

In 1959, Robert left Alcatraz and was sent to the minimum-security Medical Center for Federal Prisoners in Springfield, Missouri. He spent the last few years of his life there, and he died the day before President John F. Kennedy's assassination in 1963. While on Alcatraz, Robert wrote two books, one of which was published after his death, *Looking Outward: A Voice from the Grave*. Robert is buried next to his mother in Metropolis, Illinois. Robert's grave is surrounded by decorative birds, apparently left by visitors.

## Ellsworth Raymond "Bumpy" Johnson

Ellsworth Raymond Johnson was born in Charleston, South Carolina, in 1905. He had six siblings and grew up in a religious home. Ellsworth got his nickname, Bumpy, as a child because he had a bump on his head. In 1919, he moved to New York City, where his mother, sister, and brother Willie had moved earlier.

Ellsworth was a tough kid who didn't back down. While skipping school, he caught the eye of Harlem gangsters who saw his potential. He provided protection to local businesses and soon became a bodyguard. He kept wealthy, powerful, law-breaking businesspeople in Harlem safe wherever they went, including Madame Stephanie St. Claire, who ran an illegal lottery. Ellsworth had several encounters with law enforcement, which led to arrests for assault and burglary. He began spending time behind bars, sometimes for long stretches. It was serving time in Sing Sing, a prison in upstate New York, that Ellsworth met fellow inmate Harold Giuliani, former New York mayor Rudolph Giuliani's father.

Ellsworth didn't want white gangsters taking money out of Harlem. He is most famous for a turf war (a battle between two groups to control one area) he fought against another New York gangster, Dutch Schultz. The turf war ended when Charles "Lucky" Luciano, head of the Italian mafia, had Dutch killed. Ellsworth struck a deal with Charles that would keep Harlem under Ellsworth's control. This deal lasted for decades, and from the 1930s to the 1960s, Ellsworth was known as the "Godfather of Harlem."

In 1952, Ellsworth was convicted for drug trafficking and sentenced to fifteen years in prison, the longest sentence of his life. In total, Ellsworth spent twenty-six years in some of America's toughest prisons: Sing Sing, Dannemora, Leavenworth, Atlanta, and Alcatraz.

Though unlikely, some people speculate that Ellsworth helped three inmates,

Frank Morris and the Anglin Brothers, escape from Alcatraz in 1962 by providing a boat. In the early morning hours of July 7, 1968, Ellsworth died of a heart attack at a Harlem restaurant. He was only sixty-two years old.

## YOU CAN STILL SEE IT TODAY

Robert Stroud spent seventeen years on Alcatraz. Six of those years were spent in segregation in D-Block in cell forty-two, and eleven were spent in the prison hospital. This was done to protect other inmates from his violent outbursts. Both cells remain intact. The hospital isn't part of the standard prison tour, though sometimes special tour groups are still allowed to visit this area.

# CHAPTER 9
# WHY DID AL CAPONE GET SENT TO ALCATRAZ?

People ask about Al Capone more than any other person who has spent time on Alcatraz.

Alphonse "Scarface" Capone's real story is complicated by legends, lies, and exaggerated half-truths that have been retold so many times that they feel like the actual truth. Al was born in Brooklyn, New York, in 1899, the fourth of nine children, to Italian immigrant parents. His father, Gabriel, worked as a barber, and his mother, Theresa, as a seamstress. Al was just an "okay" student, but one day he got into a fight with his sixth-grade teacher, and that was the end of Al's formal schooling.

Al had a few real jobs, like candy-store clerk and bowling-alley pin boy, but he gravitated toward committing small-time crimes. He eventually became a bouncer for a criminal named Frankie Yale at the Harvard Inn, a dance hall and saloon. This job put him around even more tough guys who broke the law.

Before he turned twenty, several events happened that shaped the rest of Al's life. Always an extrovert who could take things too far, Al got involved in a violent brawl with Frank Galluccio. During the fight, Frank slashed Al across the face three times, leaving the scars that would earn him his famous nickname. (Al hated the nickname "Scarface," and in photos he often turned his face to hide the scars.) Three weeks later, in December 1918, Al married his wife, Mae. They had their only child, Albert Francis "Sonny" Capone, that same year.

Al took his young family and moved to Baltimore, where he worked as a bookkeeper. But the pay was not great, and he struggled. When an old friend and mentor, Johnny Torrio, visited Al in Baltimore and invited him to move to Chicago to help him run his criminal empire, Al said yes.

Shortly after Al arrived in Chicago, the US government passed the Eighteenth Amendment, banning the importation and sale of "intoxicating liquor." This is when organized crime really took off. Even though it was against the law, people didn't want to stop drinking, and so Johnny Torrio and Al Capone became bootleggers, illegally supplying booze to the thirsty people of Chicago and beyond. Other criminal gangs fought for territory with Al and Johnny, and the murders that resulted were called "the Beer Wars."

Working as a top lieutenant for Johnny in "the Outfit" wasn't the only thing keeping Al busy. His father, Gabriel, died suddenly of a heart attack at age fifty-four. Al's mother and six of his siblings decided to make their way to Chicago. Some of his brothers came to work for Al.

Reading the newspaper headlines, it looked like violent criminals were shooting other lawbreakers every week in the Chicago area. Johnny Torrio was shot five times and barely escaped with his life. Al was ambushed while overseeing business at the Hawthorne Hotel. It was a bloody time for Chicago.

To keep public opinion on his side, Al gave interviews to newspapers and magazines across the country, including the *New York Times* and *Cosmopolitan*. Al even created a soup kitchen to feed the city's poor. He loved attention, and he believed that the people loved him, too. Of course, Al always denied killing anybody and often listed his profession as a furniture salesman. Other gangsters, particularly those in New York, wanted Al to stop giving interviews. But Al was built for show. He wore flashy suits, lived very publicly and extravagantly, and resisted the low-profile lifestyles of the gangsters who came before him.

In 1925, Johnny left for Europe and turned everything over to Al. Overnight, Al became one of the most powerful crime bosses in America, and he was only twenty-six years old. Al didn't know it yet, but public opinion was about to turn against him.

Al spent a lot of money on food, clothes, travel, and family. On horse races. On dog races. On hitmen. On lawyers. On paying off officials. On his new mansion in Palm Island. Living like a celebrity wasn't a crime. But the federal government worked slowly and methodically to trap Al, who was very slippery when it came to financial transactions, for failure to pay income tax. They had convicted his brother Ralph of that crime and sent him to Leavenworth. Al had to be a little worried.

On Valentine's Day 1929, in Miami, Al went to a Dade County office building to answer questions about the recent murder of his old boss Frankie Yale in New York. But the questions they asked him weren't about Frankie; they were about Al's finances. Overconfident as usual, Al went to the meeting without an attorney. At this exact moment, as a stenographer recorded his answers, a mass murder was taking place in Chicago that would change everything for Al. By the time Al exited the interview, news of the mass slaughter was spreading quickly. Seven unarmed men, including five bootleggers, a very unlucky optometrist, and a garage mechanic, were gunned down in a garage in Chicago. Photographs of their bodies were splashed across newspapers with sensational headlines. Everyone assumed that a murder of such violence in Chicago could only have happened under Al's direction. But one victim, Frank Gusenberg, survived long enough to give a statement. When asked by a responding police sergeant who was responsible, he said, "Cops did it."

Witnesses reported a police car at the scene and two police officers among the group who entered, but people believed that it was merely criminals impersonating police to catch the victims off guard. The impact the St. Valentine's Day Massacre had on Al Capone is undeniable. Al thought his airtight alibi and actual innocence would protect him, but he was wrong.

Since there was no evidence linking Al to the St. Valentine's Day Massacre, there was no way to prosecute him for the crime. This was also true for the bootlegging and other more violent crimes. Failure to pay taxes, though, was a crime the government could prove. Al had never filed income tax returns. He didn't even have a bank account. When the government made a case for tax evasion against him, Al had very good lawyers to get him off or cut a deal. But the US government didn't want to cut a deal with Capone. They wanted him behind bars.

Al never wanted to go to trial. They had a plea deal worked out where he would plead guilty, pay his tax debt, and serve two and a half years in prison. But it was an election year for President Herbert Hoover, and he wanted Al Capone tried publicly. A high-ranking government official went and met with Judge James Wilkerson two days before the plea was to be accepted. Nobody knows exactly what was said, but two days later, the judge told Al's legal team that he wasn't going to agree to the plea deal after all, and he would sentence Al for however long he thought necessary. Al and his attorneys were shocked. Even George E. Q. Johnson, the state's attorney, couldn't believe it. Facing an unknown prison sentence, Al withdrew his guilty plea, and Judge James set a trial date.

The trial went terribly for Al. He spent time and money paying off a jury, but his friend and government informant Eddie O'Hare called the IRS agent Frank Wilson and told him about the payoffs. Moments before the trial started, Judge James asked the jury to leave, and he swapped it with a different jury in the building who hadn't been bribed. Al faced thirty-two years in prison and $80,000 in fines.

Capone's trial started on October 5, 1931, and ended on October 17 when a jury found him guilty on just five of the twenty-three charges. Al seemed relieved, but he shouldn't have been. He'd been found guilty on three felony charges. Judge James sentenced him to ten years in federal prison and one and a half years in county jail, and fined him $50,000. Al was immediately taken into custody. At thirty-two years old with a wife and young son, Al wouldn't be free again until he was forty and Sonny was in college.

When Al got sentenced, he figured he'd get sent to Leavenworth like his brother Ralph. But Al was sent to Atlanta. While there, he found a way to make the system bend to his needs. Warden David Moneypenny insisted that Al always received equal treatment with other prisoners, but when Warden Moneypenny was caught driving one of Al's Cadillacs in Illinois, this began to seem doubtful.

Reports trickled out of the prison nearly weekly that Al was given special treatment. Some of it was true. Some of it wasn't. (He wasn't wearing silk pajamas. But he was bribing officials and meeting with his friends.) This bothered government officials. So did all the front-page stories of other high-profile prisoners escaping federal prisons in dramatic breakouts. The US Department of Justice was in the process of building a maximum-security, minimum-privilege facility to punish the worst criminals in the system, and they wanted to put Al there as soon as they could.

After spending two years in Atlanta, Al was transferred to Alcatraz in 1934 in the first shipment of prisoners. Forty-three prisoners were loaded onto a specially designed and heavily fortified railcar and shackled to their seats. In Tiburon, California, all three railcars were transferred onto a barge, keeping the men shackled inside. The barge headed across the water to Alcatraz. Al became one of the few people to ever arrive at Alcatraz by train. Once there, he was issued the prison number eighty-five. Warden James Johnston was known as Saltwater Johnston, and he did not bend to Al. He treated him exactly like he treated the other prisoners.

After requesting many, many times to be allowed extra visits by nonfamily members and being denied by Warden Johnston, Al famously said, "It looks like Alcatraz has got me licked." Based on prison records, it's clear that Al tried to be a model prisoner. He worked hard, read a lot, and learned to play the mandola. And he joined the Alcatraz prison band, "The Rock Islanders." Initially he learned to play the tenor banjo but bought the more expensive eight-stringed mandola so he could play solo songs.

Unlike other prisoners who checked out popular western novels and escape stories, according to his library card, Al checked out books that could teach him something: *Practical Flower Gardening*, *How to Enjoy Music*, *Common Errors in English Corrected*, *Rudiments of Music*, *Sailing Alone Around the World*, and *Life Begins at Forty*. He also subscribed to over eighty newspapers and magazines.

Al took his work assignments seriously. His first job was in the prison laundry, but he later worked in the library and then mopped floors. Al hated prison. It's clear from the letters he wrote home that he missed his family. Al didn't know it yet, but things were about to get much, much worse for him.

On Saturday, February 5, 1938, Al's world changed forever. Instead of wearing his normal prison clothes to breakfast, he showed up in his dress-blue prison clothes, which were only worn on holidays and on Sundays. A guard sent him back to his cell to change. After changing and getting some coffee, Al got sick and couldn't speak clearly. Al had a very serious virus. He'd had it since he was twenty-two years old.

Prison officials already knew that Al was sick because it had shown up in a blood test given to him when he was admitted to the prison system. Now that he was showing severe symptoms, they did another test and found that the virus was affecting his brain. His condition worsened. He grew more confused and sometimes violent. He bashed another inmate in the head with a bedpan.

Warden Johnston kept Al in the hospital instead of the general population because of his poor health. His family in Chicago grew very worried about him. The press reported that Alcatraz had cracked Al and made him lose his mind. The newspapers didn't know about the virus. Al left Alcatraz on January 7, 1939. He was transferred to another prison to serve out his remaining sentence. On November 16, 1939, Al was released to his family, but he was too sick to go home. While in prison, Al's criminal empire had moved on without him. Prohibition had ended years earlier.

Al's family took him to a hospital in Baltimore, where he stayed for several months. When he left the hospital, Al spent most of his time at his house in Palm Island, Florida, with his family. Al never paid the taxes he owed, which totaled nearly $300,000. Al died on January 25, 1947. He was only forty-eight years old. To this day, people still think that Al Capone was the mastermind behind the St. Valentine's Day Massacre.

Al always claimed he had nothing to do with this crime. He was probably telling the truth.

## YOU CAN STILL SEE IT TODAY

Al Capone's cell is unmarked. Before he was housed in the prison hospital, he was kept in cell B-181 (It's in B-Block.). But the cells have been renumbered, so you need to look for what is now called cell B-206. That's Al Capone's cell.

# CHAPTER 10
# ARE THERE REALLY DUNGEONS UNDER ALCATRAZ?

Yes. Below A-Block and D-Block, there are a set of stairs that lead to eight cells often called the dungeon. They were mostly used during the military era of the fort. When they turn off the lights, it's so dark you can't see your own hand in front of your face. Records show only twenty-six men were kept there during the federal penitentiary years. At that time, they were referred to as "lower solitary" or "basement solitary." They're made out of basement rooms left over from the Citadel, and the conditions in which the prisoners were kept down there are pretty dismal: No outside light. No running water. Prisoners were given a bathroom bucket they had to find and use in total darkness. These cells were always damp, had no fresh air or ventilation, had cement floors, and no bedding was provided to prisoners. Food was restricted, and many inmates reported only receiving bread and water. And according to Warden James Johnston's memoir, sometimes the men were chained to the bars at the front of the cell to prevent them from breaking out.

The first prisoner sent to the dungeon was Leo McIntosh, who spent seventeen dark days there for refusing to follow Warden Johnston's strict rule of silence (no talking except during rec yard and mealtimes).

When an inmate was nearing a transfer to a different prison, a guard might lead them down the stairs in D-Block for other inmates to see but then bring him up in A-Block. It was a type of torture for inmates to see their friends being taken down the stairs and never seen again. Everyone knew there were dungeons down there. If a convict was then transferred to another prison and never seen on the island again, people wondered: Where had the prisoner who had been taken down the stairs gone?

## YOU CAN STILL SEE IT TODAY

You can see the stairs that lead to the dungeons during your cell house tour. Some people have been lucky enough to visit the dungeons. If you somehow manage it, you'll need to wear a hard hat and sign a special registry before you go down below. This is so they have an accurate number of how many bodies to search for in case there's an earthquake while you're in lower solitary. If you make it down there, look for the seventeen hash marks carved into the bricks by former convict Leo McIntosh. He counted the number of days that he was held in the dungeon. From 1934 to 1937, all prisoners were required to follow the rule of silence on Alcatraz.

SEPT 8 1934
DAYS |||||||/||/||/||||

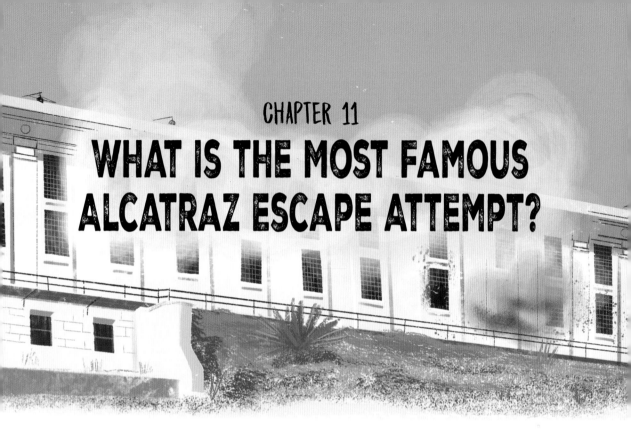

# CHAPTER 11
# WHAT IS THE MOST FAMOUS ALCATRAZ ESCAPE ATTEMPT?

People are obsessed with Alcatraz escape stories. Alcatraz was known as an escape-proof prison, but Alcatraz was not escape proof. Convicts equipped with enough determination, imagination, and opportunity found ways to maneuver themselves off the island. Sometimes they did this by using deadly force. The most well-known escape attempts are the Battle of Alcatraz (1946) and the Frank Morris/Anglin Brothers escape (1962). The first was the bloodiest revolt on Alcatraz Island.

The waters that surround Alcatraz are very, very cold. They also have strong tidal currents and a constant inflow from the Sacramento River. Trying to swim in waters that frigid and forceful, especially at night when an inmate would need the cover of darkness to escape, would quickly result in hypothermia.

Roughly speaking, depending on his overall health, an escaped prisoner could survive anywhere from one to six hours in waters this cold. But what if a person took cold showers to acclimate their body to colder water? Well, the prison officials thought of that. They were so worried about it that the prison showers always ran hot. While hot showers might be seen as a luxury in other penitentiaries, the prisoners on Alcatraz got them to keep their bodies accustomed to warm water.

Another way prison officials discouraged escape attempts was to encourage the prisoners' fear of sharks. One prisoner said that when he landed on the dock, a guard told him that they regularly fished out the sharks, cut off their left fins, and dumped them back in the bay. With only one fin, these hungry sharks weren't able to swim straight and get back to the ocean. All they could do was circle the island. It isn't true, but it did make prisoners think twice.

A last deterrent prison officials used was the fear of getting caught. Trying to escape was about the worst thing a prisoner could do. As punishment, you were either shot on sight or recaptured and put in the hole, one of six cells at the end of D-Block where prisoners were either stripped naked or to their underwear, forced to use a hole in the floor for a toilet, and kept in darkness—for a very, very, very long time. This made escape attempts extra risky. But not impossible.

On May 2, 1946, a group of six inmates executed a plan to obtain weapons so they could free themselves from the main cell house. Part of this plan worked, which made what happened next even deadlier. The convict who led this conspiracy was Bernard "Bernie" Coy, a World War I veteran turned bank robber who had a difficult time adjusting to prison. He started fights, disobeyed rules, and got caught trying to slice through a steel window guard in the bakeshop.

After being punished, Bernie returned to the general population. He didn't pick fights anymore. Even with his meager education, he became an enthusiastic reader. He also began painting. His landscapes and wartime paintings were exhibited in Washington, DC, at the Congress for the American Prison Association. His good behavior led to him to receive sought-after jobs. In Alcatraz, jobs were seen as rewards because they got you out of your cell. In Bernie's case, he was both a prison orderly (custodial work) and library orderly (he delivered books to inmates), which meant he could move about the cell house freely.

Bernie used this time to study the habits of the prison officials and look for weaknesses. He also traveled the prison, carefully selecting his accomplices. He chose Marvin Hubbard, who worked late cleanup in the prison kitchen. Marvin had a reputation as an escape artist. He grew up in extreme poverty and dropped out of grade school to work on the family farm. He'd been sent to federal prison for armed robbery, kidnapping, and murder.

Bernie didn't plan to stay on Alcatraz. At his sentencing, he'd told the judge that there was no place that could hold him. After carefully surveying the prison, Bernie decided that the weak point was the west end gun gallery. Guards didn't carry guns on the cell house floor, but armed officers were positioned on an elevated catwalk, inaccessible to the prisoners, behind iron-rod barriers. For his escape plan to work, Bernie needed to gain access to the gun gallery, obtain weapons, take hostages, and escape by boat.

Bernie went on a strict diet, losing twenty pounds, and he began working out in his cell to gain strength. With help from other inmates, he'd made a bar spreader, capable of widening the distance between the bars of the gun gallery. He practiced great patience and hid the bar spreader away until he needed it.

On the day of the escape attempt, the morning routine ran smoothly. Prisoners were awoken by the 6:30 a.m. bell, and by 7:00 a.m., they were marching to the mess hall for breakfast. After breakfast, they were marched back to their cells and got ready for their work assignments. Then they stood in silence for a head count.

Everything seemed to unfold like a normal day. Officer Bert Burch lowered key number 107 from the gun gallery to Officer William Miller so he could unlock the heavy steel door that led to the recreation yard.

The door to the industries buildings across the yard was unlocked using a similar routine. And so the inmates left for their various jobs. Once they were in the industries buildings, Officer William was supposed to send the key back to Officer Bert. For security reasons, the officer in the cell house was never supposed to keep key number 107. But Bernie noticed that Officer William didn't always follow the rules. At 11:30 a.m., a steam whistle blew, informing the inmates it was time to return to the cell house for lunch. They passed through two different metal detectors in order to return to their cells. The strict routine and controls were meant to keep everybody safe.

After lunch, after the eating utensils were counted, and after the prisoners returned to work, it was time to feed the more troublesome inmates in D-Block. Bernie swept up. A cart of food traveled past him. He watched Officer Ernest Lageson leave the prison for his lunch. At this moment, Bernie set off to the kitchen to signal Marvin. In preparation for the next phase, Marvin slid a butcher knife up his sleeve. He asked to leave. He then proceeded to the cell house, where he would receive a pat down from Officer William. Bernie swept closer to the two men. Marvin lifted his arms. Bernie grabbed Officer William from behind, and Marvin pummeled him with his fists. The inmates had timed things perfectly. Nobody was there to help Officer William.

Bernie and Marvin dragged the officer to cell number 404. Bernie pulled the key ring from the officer's belt clip. Having watched the prison operations for years, Bernie knew which levers in the control box to pull in order to open and close specific cell doors. He and Marvin took William's clothes and tied him up. Other inmates passed by, and Bernie shoved them into the cell with the unconscious officer, too. Then Bernie raced to the control box and opened three more cell doors, releasing three more of his accomplices: Miran "Buddy" Thompson, Joseph Cretzer, and Clarence Carnes, the youngest Alcatraz inmate.

Bernie had picked the perfect crew. Buddy had racked up eight successful escapes on his prison record. Joseph had tried to escape Alcatraz before by taking prison guards hostage. And Clarence, an eighteen-year-old Choctaw who grew up in rural Oklahoma, had been convicted of first-degree murder for killing a gas station attendant when he was fifteen. He was the kind of person who stood his ground. They all had a strong desire to be out of prison. Once out of his cell, Sam Shockley, an unstable prisoner, also joined the men, but several firsthand convict accounts insist Sam didn't help plan the breakout.

Once his friends were free, Bernie dashed to where he kept his bar spreader. Then he stripped down to his underwear and slathered himself in axle grease. He climbed into the west end gun gallery, placed the bar spreader between two bars, and created an opening wide enough that he could squeeze through. Bernie grabbed a riot club and waited for Officer Bert to return. As Officer Bert approached, Bernie swung the metal door forward, knocking him back.

Then Bernie took Officer Bert's guns. He lowered a pistol to Joseph, along with a large ring of keys that he was sure would hold key number 107, which provided access to the rec door and a pathway to freedom. Bernie grabbed Officer Bert's rifle and fifty rounds of ammunition. For the first time in the history of Alcatraz, the prisoners were armed with guns. He trained his gun on the next officer who walked into the cell house and put him in cell number 404. Then Bernie opened all the other prison cells, except for the isolation cells, which would have triggered an alarm.

Bernie and Joseph took the key ring and looked for key number 107. They couldn't find it. They didn't have a lot of time. They planned to overtake the prison supply boat arriving at 2:00 p.m. to escape the island. They began to panic and tried a key that wasn't number 107 in an attempt to force the lock. The door didn't open. They'd planned to get into the rec yard undetected and shoot out all the guard towers so they could make it to the dock. If they were discovered, their plan would fall apart. Another prison officer entered the cell house, was intercepted, and taken to cell number 404.

Bernie and Joseph were furious. They demanded that Officer William give them the key. Officer William had gone off script from the prison rules, and instead of returning the key, he had kept it in his shirt pocket. Bernie and Marvin had overlooked it earlier when they stripped the officer of his pants and jacket. Officer William lied and insisted the key must be in the gun gallery. Another officer entered the cell house and was quickly ushered into the cell. Officer William passed the key to this officer. And this officer placed the key in the toilet. When nobody was looking, he submerged his hand in the bowl and pushed the key back as far as he could.

Bernie decided to empty cell number 404 and search for the key. After aggressively searching the hostages, he moved them to cell number 403. Meanwhile, in the basement, Officer Ed Stucker was supervising the inmate barbers who were giving haircuts to others. When two inmates were done and asked to use the rec yard, Officer Ed agreed. They tried to access the cell house, but there wasn't an officer posted at the steel-mesh access door. When they returned, Officer Ed went upstairs. He noticed the unmanned access door. Something wasn't right. He padlocked the door as an extra safety measure and raced back downstairs. Officer Ed called Officer Cliff Fish at the armory and reported there was a serious problem in the cell house.

Officer Cliff tried to contact the officers. Phones rang throughout the cell house. Nobody picked up. Officer Cliff contacted Lieutenant Joseph Simpson. Lieutenant Joseph contacted Mail Officer Bob Baker and Records Officer Carl Sundstrom. They went to the armory and asked Officer Cliff for an update. He said he hadn't heard anything but feared the worst. Lieutenant Joseph wanted to check things out. Officer Cliff cautioned against entering the cell house. They didn't listen. Lieutenant Joseph, Officer Bob, and Officer Carl were all quickly captured by the prisoners and placed in a cell.

Officer Cliff phoned the hospital, which was upstairs from the cell house. They were unaware of any trouble. They secured their area. Officer Ed in the basement moved the inmates to the band room and secured that as well. Upstairs, Bernie and Joseph continued to tear apart cell number 404. Bernie looked at the toilet. He reached his hand all the way inside and found key number 107. Bernie handed it to Buddy, who inserted the correct key into the lock. But the door wouldn't open.

For all his planning, the one thing Bernie didn't know was that the lock was designed to jam if too many keys had already been inserted. Each twist of the wrong key had bent the tumblers, destroying the lock. Nobody would be able to escape through that door. Officer Cliff finally called Warden James Johnston at 2:00 p.m. By then Bernie had to know he'd missed his boat off the island. Warden Johnston told Officer Cliff to phone all the guard towers. He'd meet him in the armory. This left Officer Cliff a terrible choice: Should he activate the siren? Doing so would alert the world that there was a problem on Alcatraz because everybody in San Francisco would hear it. Once active, it blared for three minutes. There was no way to turn it off. The alarm would draw the prison attention and criticism. At 2:07 p.m., Officer Cliff pressed the activation key.

Bernie didn't want to give up. He raced to windows, knocked out the glass, took aim with his stolen rifle, and shot at the tower guards. The shots could be heard in San Francisco, all the way across the bay.

Bernie, Joseph, and Marvin pledged they wouldn't be taken alive. But Clarence and Buddy decided to give up. They went back to their cells. Sam did the same. The escape plan had failed, and they were finished. Officer Ernie took a pencil from his pocket and carefully wrote the names of the prisoners responsible for the prison takeover on the wall. He circled the names of those he thought were most responsible. Officers Harold Stites and Joe Maxwell tried to enter the cell house through the west gun gallery but were met by gunfire and retreated.

To take back control of the cell house, Warden Johnston felt they needed an assault team. Vessels from the Coast Guard, Navy, and San Francisco Police were now patrolling the bay. Warden Johnston sent a group of eight officers into the cell house to rescue the officers in both cells.

Bernie and Joseph waited for them. As soon as they crept into range, the two men opened fire, and a gun battle began.

More help arrived when guards from San Quentin landed on the island. Warden Johnston decided that they would send in another assault team to rescue the hostages. Almost as soon as the second assault team entered the cell house, they were fired upon. This time, they didn't back down and returned fire, desperately looking for their fellow officers.

They finally found them and began pulling the wounded men from the cells. When a prison launch arrived, it sped them to San Francisco, where ambulances awaited.

But the Battle for Alcatraz was about to enter a new level of violence. Officers had dropped gas grenades into the prison from the roof, but they fell wildly and bounced away from their intended targets. To solve this problem, they brought in a WWII hero and bunker buster named Charles Buckner. In combat, he'd learned a more precise technique. He suspended the avocado-size explosives on long pieces of wire through ventilator shafts to the cellblock. He then pulled back on the wire to expel the pins. Over and over. Nearly five hundred grenades were lowered into the cell house and detonated.

From the lawn, marines and guards fired rifle grenades into the cell house. Cots were brought to the island so the officers could rest. At 7:00 a.m., Alcatraz received the word that Officer William had died. All the other officers, even those in serious condition, were expected to survive. By 11:00 a.m., they still hadn't taken back control. Journalists watched events unfold from boats offshore, shocked by the violence. Warden Johnston began planning a third attempt to enter the prison.

The innocent prisoners inside tried to seek any kind of cover from the violent barrage of gunfire and shrapnel. Robert "Birdman" Stroud, at great risk to himself, exited his cell and, like a fifty-six-year-old trapeze artist, swung down two tiers of cells, making it to the cell house floor level. Once there, he raced to shut every steel door in D-Block to protect the helpless inmates trapped in their heavily bombed cells. Later that day, at about 1:00 p.m., an officer heard Robert yell and beg them to stop bombing the cell house before people were unnecessarily killed. He pleaded with officials and said that the armed inmates had left D-Block.

Lieutenant Philip Bergen yelled back to the prisoners that the shooting would stop but warned them to remain in their cells if they wanted to stay safe. At this point, many prisoners had left their cells and were barricaded under water-soaked mattresses. They were afraid to leave the safety of their barricade to go anywhere. The officials suspected the armed inmates were positioned in the utility corridor. Gunfire from inside the prison had stopped, and Warden Johnston felt they'd gained back control of part of the prison.

During the two-day battle, prisoners had been sleeping and living in the rec yard. Now prison officials were prepared to move these prisoners back into A-Block. Shortly before 9:00 a.m., they were ready to enter the C-Block utility corridor, where they suspected they would find Bernie, Joseph, and Marvin. They shined a light and yelled a warning into the corridor. They didn't get a response. The grenades had burst pipes, and water and raw sewage dripped from the wrecked plumbing. Guards advanced slowly through the dark and flooded walkway. They discovered Bernie first. Near him was Joseph. They'd been dead for hours. Last they found Marvin at the end of the passageway, his body still warm.

Clarence, Buddy, and Sam were brought out of their cells. They would go on trial for what they had done. No one would ever be the same again. In D-Block, you could hear the wind hiss and sing through the mortar holes. In the days that followed, funerals were held for Officer William and Officer Harold. Marvin's body was taken back to Oklahoma to be buried. Joseph was cremated and placed in a burial vault in Colma, California. Nobody claimed Bernie's remains. He was buried in an unmarked grave in a simple pine coffin in Colma.

In the weeks that followed, Clarence, Buddy, and Sam were put on trial for their lives for the murder of Officer William. Robert "Birdman" Stroud donated $200 to the prisoners' defense, and many other prisoners testified on their behalf. Many convicts felt that Sam was unfairly tried and stated that on the witness stand. The trial lasted a month. In the end, Sam and Buddy were given the death penalty. They were executed together, side by side, in the gas chamber in San Quentin on September 24, 1948, almost two and a half years after their violent escape attempt. Neither man had last words.

Clarence was returned to Alcatraz after being locked on the mainland for the trial. Decades later, after Alcatraz opened as a tourist attraction, Clarence spent time talking about his prison experience and worked with a Hollywood production about his life that aired on television in 1980.

Clarence died on October 3, 1988, at the Medical Center for Federal Prisoners in Springfield, Missouri, and was buried in a pauper's grave. One good friend Clarence had made in Alcatraz was the notorious mobster James "Whitey" Bulger. When Whitey heard about Clarence's death, he paid for Clarence's body to be exhumed and buried in the Choctaw Nation of Oklahoma. Clarence was laid to rest a second time, between his brother and sister, at the Billy Cemetery in Daisy, Oklahoma.

## YOU CAN STILL SEE IT TODAY

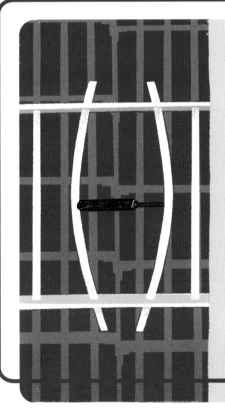

During the Battle of Alcatraz, when marines drilled holes into the prison's ceiling and detonated grenades, they left permanent marks in the concrete floor that you can still see today. As you enter the cut off, a pass-through area between cellblocks, you can see the patched-up scars. There is a bar spreader on display, and the prison has marked the place where Bernie Coy gained entry into the gun gallery. Cell number 404 has been turned into a permanent memorial for Officer William.

# CHAPTER 12

# DID ANYONE EVER ESCAPE BY RAFT?

To this day, visitors are obsessed with the 1962 escape of Frank Morris and the Anglin brothers, Clarence and John.

In 1962, Alcatraz was under the control of its fourth warden, Olin Guy Blackwell. The prison was in decline, and Warden Blackwell had to make the prison run on less money than all the wardens before him had. Warden Blackwell transformed the dining area from ten-man tables to four-man tables, which meant four convicts could have private conversations, possibly plotting an escape and possibly stealing stainless-steel utensils, such as a spoon, to help chip away cement from a cell's vent, without worrying about a snitch at their table. That's exactly what Frank, Clarence, John, and Allen West did.

Most people who've studied the escape think it was Allen West, serving his second term at Alcatraz, who came up with the initial escape plan. Allen had been a criminal his entire life. Born in New York City into a poor family, Allen had become a car thief by the time he was fourteen.

When Allen arrived at Alcatraz for the first time in 1954, Warden Edwin Swope oversaw the island. Warden Swope was the only warden in the history of the island not to have an escape attempt while in that role. Under his leadership, because of budget cuts, the prison made many changes. They decreased the manned guard towers from six to four. They decreased mail censoring for incoming mail and magazines. They closed the east gun gallery, greatly reducing nighttime surveillance in the cell house. Allen was twenty-five years old, a known escape risk, and had already been locked up for nine years of his life. He was always looking for a prison's soft spots.

Allen spent two tough years on Alcatraz before getting transferred back to the federal prison in Atlanta, Georgia. While there, he became friendly with Frank Morris, who was serving out a long fourteen-year sentence. Clarence and John Anglin were also in that prison. Violent, and ever-resourceful, in 1957, Allen escaped from prison in Georgia. In 1958, Allen became one of the rare prisoners to receive a second Alcatraz inmate number. In 1954, he'd received inmate number 1130. In 1958, he became inmate number 1335.

Allen stirred up trouble the first years after he returned to Alcatraz and spent a lot of well-earned time in solitary. Frank Morris was thirty-three years old and had spent almost twenty years of his life behind bars when he arrived at Alcatraz in January 1960. Born in New York City in 1926, Frank had a very unstable childhood. He was in and out of foster care until he ran away from home at age eleven, the same year his mother died. An orphan without any relatives, Frank never had any visitors or received any mail while in Alcatraz.

In October 1960, John Anglin arrived on Alcatraz. Three months later, his younger brother Clarence joined him there. John and Clarence were born one year apart, into a family with fourteen children, to parents who worked as traveling farmers, moving the family north to pick cherries in Michigan or south to pick tomatoes in Florida. Neither made it through elementary school. Small crimes escalated to a big one, and a bank robbery they committed in Columbia, Alabama, with a third brother, Alfred, landed them in federal prison and then in Alcatraz.

Frank's first job was in the library, which meant he had the freedom to move around the cell house. It was there that the escape plot began. Allen West approached the other three men while working his cell house job. He already had much of the escape imagined. They'd create models that resembled real heads and put them in their beds. They wouldn't make the same mistake as the 1939 escape group. Allen knew the only reason they didn't make it was because those men had been discovered missing. He said confidently that he'd found a ceiling vent that could serve as their escape hatch to the roof. All four men were excited about the plan; Frank Morris probably the most.

Allen talked about his escape plan for more than a year, sometimes while in segregation, through his toilet to other convicts (pipes with the water removed could carry voices), imagining his options. Maybe they could seize the dock boat. Maybe they could bind driftwood together. Maybe they could take hostages or even inflate surgical gloves to buoy themselves and swim to shore. Allen was released from segregation on May 5, 1961. He was assigned to cell B-152, three floors directly below the ceiling vent he'd heard could lead to the roof.

There were 336 cells on Alcatraz, but usually the prison only held around 250 inmates, so there were always empty cells. The convicts were allowed to request cells and be transferred (though sometimes they were moved involuntarily for bad behavior). In his two and a half years on the island, Frank had moved cells six times.

In his four years on the island, Allen had moved cells twenty-nine times. Once out of segregation, Allen crossed paths with John Anglin in the cafeteria and invited him to join the plan. Without consulting the others, John invited his brother Clarence to join, too. Frank was assigned to cell B-138. Clarence and John were in cells B-140 and B-142, even though their files warned prison staff not to house the brothers near each other. Being so close allowed the inmates to communicate easily about their upcoming breakout. In addition to talking at meals, or on the weekends in the recreation yard, Frank, Allen, John, and Clarence could whisper to one another in their cells. They also communicated during music hour, a new program Warden Blackwell had started that allowed prisoners to play instruments in their cells for one hour each night. The crew benefited tremendously from this nightly music hour as their plans unfolded.

Out of segregation and eligible to work again, Allen was offered a job perfectly suited for a prisoner creating an escape plan: working inside the cell house on a maintenance crew. That summer, he repainted cells and other parts of the prison. Guards would unlock A-Block for him, a corridor of cells that the prison staff used as a supply area. It was a place where he could steal tools and materials without anybody noticing.

One bit of luck the four inmates had on their side was the aging plumbing system. All the toilets in the prison used highly corrosive salt water, which was hard on the pipes. There'd been a request to replace the plumbing in 1949, but that never happened. For more than fifty years, these pipes had been bursting, sometimes flooding the utility corridor behind the cells. When this happened, the salt water and sewage would seep into the concrete walls, weakening them. Multiple pipe bursts in 1960 and '61 required the help of a convict plumber named Billy Boggs, who happened to be housed in a cell near Allen. When Billy fixed the pipes, he also surveyed the utility corridor directly behind their cells and realized a convict could climb the pipes like a ladder to the roof. He most definitely mentioned this to Allen. Some interviews suggest that Billy might have been in on the plan for a while.

Cautious and probably a little nervous about trusting Allen completely, Frank requested a cell transfer to the third tier, directly below the ceiling vent they planned to use in the escape. Once he was satisfied it was a possible path to freedom, he requested a cell transfer to the first floor B-138. Allen made a request and moved to B-140. John and Clarence requested to move to B-152 and B-150. For months, most likely using steel spoon handles stolen from the cafeteria, they chipped away at the cement around the vents at the back of their cells. While other convicts would flirt with the idea of joining the escape plot, only Allen, Frank, John, and Clarence remained fully committed to the plan.

Their rough plan included digging out of the backs of their cells, leaving fake heads in their beds, climbing up the pipes in the utility corridor to the roof, prying open the ceiling vent, climbing onto the roof, shinnying down the bakery smokestack to the water, and somehow making it to shore. And once the idea of using a raft emerged, the prisoners' work intensified.

Frank liked to read magazines, and two issues of *Popular Mechanics* (that can still be found in the Parks Archives and Record Center in the Presidio in San Francisco) were critical for making the raft they used in the escape. A November 1960 article titled "Rubber Geese" discussed how to make goose decoys out of inner tubes and further explained how anybody can vulcanize, or chemically treat, the seams of rubber using heat and glue to make a watertight bond.

A second article appeared in March 1962, just weeks before the escape. "Your Life Preserver—How Will It Behave If You Need It?" provided photos of a variety of life vests and ways to wear them. This issue was found during a search of Frank's cell after the escape. Perhaps it was this article that inspired the men to construct four life preservers out of raincoats, in addition to their raft.

It wasn't an accident that Frank ended up with these magazines. At the onset of the escape planning, he made a magazine-subscription request in his own handwriting for five magazines: *Popular Science*, *Popular Mechanics*, *Mechanix Illustrated*, *Science Digest*, and probably to look less suspicious, a subscription to *Chess Review*.

The convicts needed a hidden space to assemble and store the fourteen-foot by six-foot raft. Allen approached the prison guards about possibly hanging some blankets above the third tier of cells, essentially an unused, barred gap with plenty of clearance to stand up in between the cells themselves and the cell house ceiling. He argued that while he worked in that area painting and cleaning, the blankets would prevent debris from spilling onto the area below. After initially being told no, Allen finally convinced somebody on staff to say yes. These blankets concealed the men's workshop and allowed them to exit their cells at night to work on loosening the overhead vent and store their raft.

Some speculate the men used stolen spoons with sharpened handles to drill a series of holes around their vents. Others pointed out that these holes were too perfectly round, and they were instead made by a diamond drill bit. Where would the men have gotten electricity to use a homemade drill in their cells? Maybe from the wiring from their prison cells' single light bulbs. However the men dug these holes, they carefully tucked the dust, pebbles, and pieces of cement in their pockets and disposed of that when they were out of their cells. As they broke away the concrete from their vents, the men realized they needed to create fake vent covers and a portion of fake wall to disguise their digging. They did this by taking cardboard binder covers, painstakingly cutting seventy diamonds to replicate the grill's pattern, and then carefully painting the fake grills the same green color as their cells. They purchased canvas board through the prison using money they earned from working their cell house jobs to construct a phony wall, and they used soap to conceal the seam. The plan was for each convict to create a false vent/wall area, which they could easily detach and reinsert once they crawled out of their cells into the utility corridor. It would make it much easier for them to exit their cells at night and climb the pipes to their work area. Though they always made sure to keep their cell neighbor on watch for them.

On April 25, John was the first to break through his cell wall. Clarence followed a couple of days later, with John helping from the utility corridor outside. Allen and Frank grew nervous. They didn't completely trust John and Clarence and didn't want them both up there without one of them. Frank broke through his wall on May 11. Allen did not fully dig out of his cell. Instead of leaving his cell to go up top to work, he assembled all four life jackets within his cell. With three exit holes fully completed and one nearly complete, the next phase of the escape began. But before the men could leave their cells to work, they needed to create their fake heads.

The four heads ended up being very different in size, shape, quality, and materials used. One was only a half head with splotchy hair and a big, thick, overly pink ear, which the men nicknamed "Oink." Three heads were made with wire, but the fourth was not. One was so artfully painted and sculpted that it earned the nickname "Oscar," after an uncle. The heads were built out of a variety of materials: cement dust, glue, plaster, cement paste, and possibly soap. They were made lifelike with oil paint and real human hair from the barbershop, courtesy of Clarence, who worked there. They even had eyebrows and eyelashes.

With the fake heads in place in their beds, Frank and Clarence, or Frank and John, would leave their cells, climb the pipes three stories to the area above the cells, and work behind the cover of the blankets during music hour. They loosened the ceiling vent and assembled their raft. Some say the convicts below, aware of the escape plan, played their instruments even louder to disguise the sound of tools working against metal.

It took time to break the vent open, but once they did, they made a fake bolt out of soap to hide what they'd done. After removing the vent, Frank discovered two reinforcing rods and an iron grate. He hadn't been expecting to run into this problem. The bars would need to be spread and the grate removed before the men could squeeze through the shaft and escape. Night after night, they made trip after trip to the top of the cells. They'd bring up many items, including a handmade pen-size flashlight and a bar spreader. They crafted a hand drill using a vacuum-cleaner motor. They took the plastic dip tubes from Windex spray bottles to create blow tubes to allow them to inflate their life vests while wearing them at sea. For Frank, getting through the grate and its many rivets was tough, tough work.

The four inmates were smuggling pieces of raincoats into the industries building, where they were stitched together on sewing machines, perhaps in the glove shop. Just like they'd read about in *Popular Mechanics* magazine, the men treated the seams with glue and also likely heated them on steampipes to create a watertight bond. The paddles were probably assembled at night on top of the cells behind the blankets. Allen began to worry about the blankets. He knew they'd have to come down soon. If they did, how and where would they assemble the raft?

They worked with urgency. Frank spent three nights spreading the bars, but that still left the grate, which had twelve rivets. They tried converting stolen barber shears and later a vacuum-cleaner motor and later a vacuum-cleaner motor, but neither were strong enough, and they made too much noise. Frank would need to pry off each rivet with a screwdriver and brute force. Once, under the strain, he dropped a tool, and it clattered all the way down three stories. Everyone had to have heard it, but shockingly, no one reacted.

Dropping the tool was one of several mistakes the four men made that could have spoiled the escape. Many other inmates knew what they were doing, and any could have squealed. Especially men on the other side of the utility corridor, who could see through their own vents directly into the cells of Allen, Frank, John, and Clarence. They'd known for months about the digging. Inmates near and around their cells also knew. But nobody ratted them out. And nobody on the prison staff figured out their plans.

Some people think that the inmates had help from the inside. But there's no evidence to support that idea. More likely, the staff thought that for a prisoner to escape the cell house, he'd need to saw through the front bars, which the guards banged on regularly with a baton to make sure they were untampered with and solid. But they didn't seem to notice that so many items had gone missing: spoons, ladles, various types of glue, saw blades, spare wood, brass screws, tape, dozens of raincoats, two homemade drills, electrical wire, files, wrenches, screwdrivers, a stapler, bolts, drill bits, and more.

Frank and Allen always had concerns that John and Clarence could double-cross them. When John and Clarence deviated from the original plan— constructing a six-foot by fourteen-foot rectangular raft—and instead omitted one of the sides to make a triangular raft, Frank and Allen worried that the new design wouldn't fit all four men. Were John and Clarence assembling a raft only big enough for two?

Frank accepted the size of the smaller raft and moved on. He continued to pry off the rivets. Frank had to semi-insert himself into the vent to finish the job, but he did it. Their escape hatch to freedom was open. Clarence handed Frank their homemade periscope, made from art board and broken pieces of mirror. Frank fed it through the vent and studied the cell house roof. He could see the beam of the lighthouse pan around the island. They could also see the absence of a guard tower, and it must have thrilled them.

They knew that they only had one more day on the island, so they took all their tools and placed them in a five-gallon drum of cement paint: the spoon handles, the electrical wire, bolts, nuts, and everything else. They wanted to hide it and hoped it would never be found. This would protect the inmates who'd helped them get these supplies. On June 11, they stood for their 7:00 a.m. wake-up call, knowing it would be their last. They spent the day pretending everything was normal.

Frank left his cell first that evening, to climb the pipes and retrieve the heads. John and Clarence exited their cells, but Allen did not. Allen hadn't dug out enough of his cell, and he couldn't get through the hole.

Frank, Clarence, and John were already on the roof.

The path the three men took to the water was clear. They left a hundred yards of footprints across the roof, leading to a smokestack that they all clung to as they dropped forty-five feet down the building's side. They most likely used electrical wire to lower down the raft, paddles, life vests, and concertina (an accordion-like instrument they planned to use to inflate the raft). This occurred between 10:30 p.m. and 10:45 p.m. They ran near the water tower, crossed a road, and flung themselves down a steep incline. Maybe to lighten their load, maybe to be kindhearted, they put a paddle and lifejacket near the vent on the roof, presumably for Allen.

The three men may have been at the shoreline by 11:00 p.m. They unrolled the raft and inflated it using the concertina as a foot pump.

Frank, John, and Clarence weren't discovered missing until the morning count at 7:00 a.m., during which they were required to stand. When Clarence didn't wake up, they sent Officer Bill Long to his cell. Officer Bill whacked the bed, and the head rolled onto the floor and broke. Whistles blew. Alarms sounded. They found Frank and John were missing, too. Because Warden Blackwell was away on a fishing trip, the acting warden at the time, Art Dollison, oversaw the search to recapture the three men. It didn't take long for the guards to follow the prisoners' path up the pipes and onto the roof. They found Allen's left-behind life vest and oar. Bloodhounds arrived from San Quentin. The scent trail led to the water.

They found the five-gallon cement can and broke it open. Guards dug through the pieces, trying to figure out how the prisoners had managed to escape. They found a similar five-gallon container in A-Block. It also held tools from the escape. Art Dollison pulled Allen away from the other convicts to interview him, and Allen quickly admitted to being the mastermind of the whole plan. He said that he had started planning the escape as soon as he was released from D-Block on May 5, 1961.

The search for the escaped convicts began quickly. FBI agents arrived on the island within the hour. To search the water, the Coast Guard sent out four patrol boats and a helicopter. The US military ended up sending nearly three dozen military police and a hundred men from Fort Baker and Angel Island. The FBI spent days going door-to-door and also searching the shoreline and looking for missing boats.

Tips, leads, and false sightings poured in, but none panned out. It was as if the three men had vanished. On the night of June 12, a paddle that matched the one found on the hospital roof was found floating off the northwest side of Angel

Island. Two days later, debris boats combing the bay found two homemade, drab-green packets caught in a whirlpool half a mile from Alcatraz. They contained Anglin family photos, a list of addresses and names to contact on the outside, and a ten-dollar receipt in Clarence's name for money deposited into his prison account. People suspected that the men wouldn't have intentionally parted with such important things and began to believe that the trio might have drowned. The next day, a life jacket matching the one left for Allen washed up on a popular beach just north of the Golden Gate. A week later, a second life jacket would be plucked from the waters near Alcatraz, and this one had blood spots on it. But what about the men? If they'd drowned, wouldn't searchers have found their bodies?

Astonishingly, Frank, John, and Clarence weren't the only people who went missing in the bay at that time. A man named Seymour Webb had jumped from the Golden Gate Bridge. And a few days later, Robert Pains drowned while swimming in Half Moon Bay, roughly twenty-five miles south of the Golden Gate Bridge. It's reported that of these five bodies, none were ever found. A theory took hold that they all had been pulled out to the Pacific Ocean by powerful spring currents. Sometimes, though, incoming tides will bring a body back. Eight months after the escape, skeletal remains were found on a nearby beach in Point Reyes. Unidentified, they were buried in a local cemetery under the name John Bones Doe. While the remains of John Bones Doe remain unidentified, DNA testing has confirmed that they do not belong to either John or Clarence. There are no known relatives for Frank to provide DNA for testing, though the bones match exactly Frank's height, sixty-seven and a half inches.

For nearly two decades, the FBI oversaw this case, but in 1979 it was handed off to the US Marshals Service. A lot of people believed that Frank, John, and Clarence drowned in the frigid bay. The raft has never been found, which seems to suggest that everything, including Frank, John, and Clarence, were pulled out to sea. For years everybody believed that the oar, the two life jackets, and the packets of photos and papers were the only items ever found in connection to the escape. But this is wrong.

Decades after the escape, it's been uncovered that a car had been stolen in Marin County on the night of the escape, a Blue 1955 Chevrolet, license plate KPB-076. Also, there was an FBI teletype dated June 12, 1962, that read "raft believed used be [sic] escapees located on Angel Island." And another report stated, "should be on the lookout for a 1955 Chevrolet blue in color, bearing California license KPB-076." Also, a San Francisco police officer claimed that he saw a boat in the water that night near Alcatraz. Could it have picked up the escapees?

The theory that all the bodies from those who went missing in those waters were never recovered also turned out to be wrong. The body of Robert Pains, the swimmer who drowned near Half Moon Bay, was recovered in shallow water and identified. Which means those currents do bring drowned bodies back to shore.

Most recently, a photograph of two men in Brazil taken in 1975 was given to a forensic facial-imaging specialist and retired police sergeant. Comparing the photograph against John's and Clarence's mugshots, he concluded it was highly likely that the two individuals in the 1975 photograph are John and Clarence Anglin. Many people dismiss this photograph. But could it be possible that two or three career criminals got off that island, survived the current and frigid water, and never again committed any crimes that would put them back in the prison system?

Frank Morris's prison papers record his IQ score at 133, near genius level. John and Clarence were strong swimmers, and while growing up they swam in the icy waters of Lake Michigan. Maybe, somehow, they survived the unsurvivable.

One thing is perfectly clear: Frank, John, and Clarence *did* escape Alcatraz.

This case and the search for the three escapees will remain active until 2030, when all three men will have reached the age of one hundred years old.

## YOU CAN STILL SEE IT TODAY

A piece of wall has been removed so the pipes that Frank, John, and Clarence climbed to escape to the roof are visible today. You can also visit their cells and see how they removed their vents to escape. Replica fake heads rest on their pillows. Frank's cell is 138, Clarence's is 152, John's is 150, and Allen's is 140.

# CHAPTER 13
# WERE ANY PRISONERS EXECUTED ON ALCATRAZ?

MORGUE
1910

The short answer is no. Executions in California occur only at the San Quentin State Prison. Since the death penalty was reinstated in 1977, thirteen people have been executed in the gas chamber there.

Perhaps the question underneath this question is, "How many people died on Alcatraz?" Sadly, a lot. Five died by suicide. Fifteen died from natural causes. Eight men were killed by other inmates. And many prisoners died while trying to escape from the island. There were fourteen different escape attempts on the island, involving a total of thirty-four men. Two men tried to escape twice: Joseph Cretzer and Sam Shockley. Seven inmates—Joseph Bowers, Thomas Limerick, Arthur "Doc" Barker, Bernie Coy, Joseph Cretzer, Marvin Hubbard, and James Boarman—were shot to death. Aaron Burgett drowned. Five men vanished: Theodore Cole, Ralph Roe, Frank Morris, Clarence Anglin, and John Anglin. Only one man managed to swim from Alcatraz to the mainland, John Paul Scott. He escaped from a kitchen window with Darl Dee Parker on December 16, 1962. John made it all the way to the rocky shore of Fort Point, where teenagers alerted authorities, who then brought him to shore near death. He was transported back to Alcatraz. John and Darl's escape would be the final attempt to break out of The Rock. Less than four months later, after twenty-nine years of operation, Alcatraz closed.

There is a small building, north of the cell house, labeled the morgue. It was built in 1910 behind the dining hall of the main prison near the top of the island, but it was only used once, to store a deceased prisoner overnight until his body could be taken to the mainland. The Bureau of Prisons eventually converted the small building to store a backup generator.

While it's true that no prisoners were executed on Alcatraz, two prisoners were executed for their role in an escape attempt. Miran "Buddy" Thompson and Sam Shockley died simultaneously in the gas chamber in San Quentin on December 3, 1948, for their roles in the deadly prison takeover in 1946, the Battle of Alcatraz.

## YOU CAN STILL SEE IT TODAY

Most visitors pass by the morgue without realizing it's there. Before you reach the basement of the cell house, you'll pass a small, white building with a fire hydrant in front of it. Look inside. That's the Alcatraz morgue.

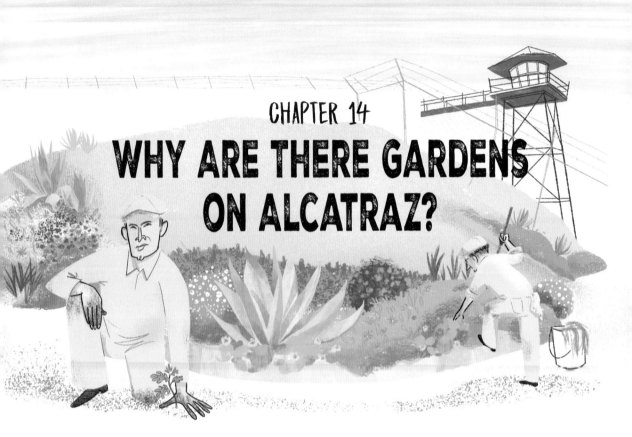

# CHAPTER 14
# WHY ARE THERE GARDENS ON ALCATRAZ?

To understand why there are gardens on Alcatraz, let's start with how the soil got there. Soon after Alcatraz was blasted into its present-day shape, Fort Alcatraz was built. The completed fort consisted of many buildings, which meant that people now worked and lived on the island. The people who lived there wanted their island home to feel less bleak, so they imported soil from nearby Angel Island and the Presidio (a military post in San Francisco where soldiers and their families once lived) to plant flower gardens and soften this barren spot. Also, because Alcatraz was a fort with cannons aimed to fire upon any ship entering the bay, the military brought soil over to help fortify the structures from potential incoming cannon fire.

Alcatraz didn't last long as a fort, but the soil remained. Other than some seeds that were transported early on with the soil, Alcatraz didn't really have any native plants. The oldest picture we have of the gardens on Alcatraz dates back to 1869. You can see military officers and their wives lounging in a large, elaborate Victorian garden beside the Citadel, the building that used to be at the top of the island. To create these compact gardens, deep holes were cut into the rock and planted with sweet peas, lilies, and roses.

It wasn't just the island inhabitants who wanted to beautify the island. In the city of San Francisco, the public worried that Alcatraz was becoming a blocky, gray eyesore. In the 1920s, more than a decade before Alcatraz would become a federal prison, the California Spring Blossom and Wildflower Association donated many pounds of seeds to help beautify the island. Military prisoners planted three hundred trees (sequoias, cypresses, and pines) and hundreds of pounds of Shirley poppy seeds, nasturtium, and shrubs. A lot of these plants died due to lack of water, wind, and scant care. But some survived.

When the federal prison opened in 1934, the secretary to the warden, Freddie Reichel, realized the value of keeping the gardens alive. Under Freddie's care, the gardens expanded. San Diego botanist and landscape architect Kate Sessions introduced Freddie to plants that grew well in challenging conditions, such as aeonium (hens and chicks), New Zealand Christmas trees, bougainvillea, and agave. Kate sent Freddie cuttings of agave and ice plants to adorn the steep west slope.

It took persistence, but Freddie finally persuaded the prison warden to let inmates garden, too. There was some controversy involved with letting the maximum-security prisoners have access to tools, including hoses and hand shovels.

Two of the most famous prison gardeners during this time were longtime criminal friends reunited on Alcatraz, Elliott Michener and Dick Franzeen.

They first met in high school at the Idaho Industrial Reform School. Both were counterfeiters and escape artists who, combined, spent decades on Alcatraz. Dick came from a farm and was handpicked by Freddie to tend to the rose garden and plants on the island's east side. Elliott arrived on Alcatraz the year Freddie left and became a gardener by being trustworthy: He dutifully collected the handballs that landed outside the rec yard walls and also returned a dropped key to a prison guard.

The gardens on the west side were built by Elliott, as was the toolshed. Dick's gardens were located on the other side of the island. Out of nothing, and without gloves, Elliott worked to improve the soil on the island's harshest side and create terraced gardens. It took him hours to break the compact dirt apart. To add nutrients, he hauled bags of kitchen waste from the incinerator. The only people who ever saw Elliott's gardens were the other prisoners or the guards who oversaw them on the west side. While Dick gave Elliott seeds and planting advice, and he exchanged cut flowers with him, neither man ever saw each other's gardens. Ever.

Elliott Michener is easily recognized as the most famous prisoner gardener on Alcatraz, probably due to interviews he gave toward the end of his life in which he discussed his work in the gardens at a time in the mid-1980s and early '90s when people had taken an interest in restoring them.

For decades, prisoners thoughtfully tended to the four and a half acres of gardens throughout the island. On March 21, 1963, Attorney General Robert F. Kennedy ordered Alcatraz closed, and the gardens were left to run wild for forty years. The National Park Service took over the island in the 1970s and began giving guided tours. Sprawling roses, blackberries, and vines had escaped their beds and provided pops of color throughout the area. In the 1990s, a landscape architect named Ron Lutsko came to the island and cataloged over 150 different surviving plants. In 2003, led by Carola Ashford, the Garden Conservancy joined with the

National Park Service and the Golden Gate National Park Conservancy to restore the gardens using historical photographs. When volunteers went in to remove the overgrown blackberry bushes, rose bushes, ivy, and weeds, they were surprised to find that such a variety of plants and flowers had survived.

One bed in particular is off to the left of the main road, just past the electric shop as you make your way from the dock to the cell house. This bed now overflows with plants that grew in spite of decades of neglect, watered only by fog drip and winter rains: fuchsia, yellow bush lupine, ice plant, hens and chicks, pelargonium, California poppies, calla lilies, and more. This is called the survivor bed. It also contains a very, very rare rose, which was at one time thought to be extinct.

When volunteers first discovered it behind the ruins of the old warden's house, they shared it with a rosarian who identified it as the Bardou Job rose, a cultivated variety grown in France. What these volunteers didn't know was, at this same time, across the Atlantic Ocean, a museum in Wales—St. Fagans National Museum of History—was trying to track down the Bardou Job rose. A hundred years ago, the flower had bloomed and flourished on their museum grounds. But then it vanished. They hoped to bring it back. Using an early rose-tracking website, the rose was soon returned to Wales and the museum from the Alcatraz garden. It's a very happy ending for a very hardy rose.

Tourists in the prisoners' gardens, surrounded by the flower beds that Elliott Michener had overseen, are reminded of this quote from Elliott: "The hillside provided a refuge from disturbances of the prison, the work a release, and it became an obsession. This one thing I would do well. . . . If we are all our own jailers, and prisoners of our traits, then I am grateful for my introduction to the spade and trowel, the seed and the spray can. They have given me a lasting interest in creativity."

Volunteer gardeners have restored five of the historic garden areas: the landscape along the main road, officers' row, the rose terrace, the cell house slope, and the prisoners' gardens. The gardens have grown so popular that sometimes visitors come to Alcatraz just to see the flowers. There is always something in bloom.

## YOU CAN STILL SEE IT TODAY

The restored gardens can be seen in many areas of the island. You'll find the survivor bed on the main road, the Bardou Job rose and its bright red petals in the rose garden. Across from the cell house is a long row of happy geraniums. Before that cement trench held flowers, it held cannonballs.

# CHAPTER 15
# WHY DID THE PRISON CLOSE?

The prison was closed in 1963 by order of Attorney General Robert F. Kennedy because it was too expensive to operate. Getting supplies to the island came with a huge price tag that couldn't be ignored. One million gallons of fresh water had to be carried by barge from the mainland every week, along with food, fuel, and other supplies. The federal prison in Atlanta performed the same function as Alcatraz at a third of the cost. And the salty sea air and constant wind had degraded the facilities. Some of the buildings were actually crumbling. It would take millions of dollars to make needed renovations to Alcatraz. During its nearly three decades in operation, Alcatraz housed 1,546 men. You might read somewhere else that it housed 1,576 men, but they are double counting inmates who got sent to Alcatraz a second time—and also counting one inmate three times. James Audett is the only prisoner to serve three commitments on Alcatraz: number 208, number 551, and number 1217. But by the early 1960s, shipping men to an island prison with basement dungeons surrounded by sharks no longer matched the mood of the country.

The entire reason Alcatraz had been built was because the Justice Department wanted to have an inescapable penitentiary. But the escape from the cell house in 1962 by Frank Morris and John and Clarence Anglin, followed by the escape later that year of Darl Dee Parker and John Paul Scott from the kitchen, had destroyed that image. Inmates *could* escape Alcatraz. And the frigid water boundary full of deadly currents wasn't as uncrossable as everybody had said they were.

The closing of Alcatraz took place over months. Small groups of prisoners were taken to San Francisco International Airport and flown to other institutions. On March 21, 1963, the day Alcatraz closed, the final twenty-seven inmates were taken off the island in handcuffs and leg and waist chains. They boarded the prison boat and headed for the airport. Frank Weatherman (number 1576), the last inmate to leave Alcatraz, said the following words as he left: "Alcatraz was never no good for nobody."

## YOU CAN STILL SEE IT TODAY

In the dining hall, the breakfast menu for March 21, 1963, remains. The prison's last meal, preserved on the hallway board:

21    MARCH    1963

ASSORTED DRY CEREALS
STEAMED WHEAT
1  SCRAMBLED EGGS
2  FRESH MILK
STEWED FRUIT
TOAST
BREAD
BUTTER
COFFEE

# CHAPTER 16
# WHEN DID INDIANS OF ALL TRIBES OCCUPY ALCATRAZ?

When I arrived on Alcatraz, I knew very little about the occupation led by Akwesasne Mohawk activist Richard Oakes that began the week before Thanksgiving 1969. How and why seventy-eight young protesters, mostly students, arrived on Alcatraz was one of the things I was asked about more and more as time went on. People seemed most familiar with the occupation that lasted nineteen months, but there are actually two earlier occupations of Alcatraz leading up to this one, which are an important part of telling the whole story.

When the prison closed on Alcatraz, the island became surplus (meaning extra) federal land, a phrase that caught the attention of a group of young Native students. At this time, the Bay Area had a robust population and strong community of young Native Americans. They were immediately aware that surplus federal land and abandoned federal property had been promised to Native Americans in various treaties. After some research, they concluded their best legal argument for taking ownership of Alcatraz was linking their claim to the Sioux and the Fort Laramie Treaty that had been signed in 1868.

The first occupation occurred on March 8, 1964, and only lasted a few hours. Forty members of various First Nations took a boat to Alcatraz and tried to claim the island for forty-seven cents an acre, the same price California had offered members of many First Nations for land claims in the prior century. Allen Cottier, a Sioux housepainter with a direct ancestorial line to Crazy Horse, an Oglala Lakota war leader, read the declaration. Adam Fortunate Eagle marched with them. The coverage that followed this event exhilarated young activists across California and beyond.

Now that the Bureau of Prisons had abandoned Alcatraz, a man from Texas, Lamar Hunt, wanted to buy the island. He wanted to build a space tower to serve as a memorial for the Apollo 8 mission and also build an amusement park. In September 1969, the city approved the sale. Local businessmen enraged by this idea ran a full-page ad in the *San Francisco Chronicle* protesting the plan, which turned public opinion against the Texas oilman. Adam Fortunate Eagle and Richard Oakes both followed Alcatraz's fate in the news.

On November 20, 1969, a group of Sausalito boat operators agreed to take the young activists to Alcatraz. As the boats dropped them at the dock, the security guard on the island shouted over the Coast Guard radio, "Mayday! Mayday! The Indians have landed." The media began reporting almost immediately about the event. More and more members of First Nations went to the island. The government's initial response was to set up a blockade to the island. They were planning to send in forces and aggressively remove the activists. But the movement had a lot of support, so instead the government changed their position and sent over a negotiator from the White House.

The protesters united and called themselves the Indians of All Tribes. They began to realize that the demonstration was going to last a long time. Richard Oakes read part of the following declaration to the media. "We will purchase said Alcatraz Island for twenty-four dollars in glass beads and red cloth, a precedent set by the white man's purchase of a similar island about three hundred years ago. We know that twenty-four dollars in trade goods for these sixteen acres is more than was paid when Manhattan Island was sold, but we know that land values have risen over the years." In addition to drawing global attention to their cause, they had a clear goal of establishing a cultural center on the island to replace the American Indian Center that had been destroyed by fire in San Francisco. They also wanted the island to house an Indian Center of Ecology, which would focus on environmental research, and a Great Indian Training School, which would sell arts and crafts and offer job training and also operate as a restaurant.

On the island, they set up an intertribal council, and John Trudell ran a radio station called Radio Free Alcatraz. At its peak, four hundred people lived on The Rock. There was enormous support for the movement, but the government didn't want to negotiate with the protesters. Weeks grew into months, and many people visited the island and brought supplies. Over time, many of the original students went back to school.

A tragedy shifted the movement's energy entirely. Richard Oakes's twelve-year-old daughter, Yvonne, died following a fall down several flights of stairs on Alcatraz. After this, Richard, his wife, and the rest of his family left the island. The occupation's outlook dimmed. The US government stopped the water barge from coming to the island. President Richard Nixon cut off all power to the island. Soon after that, a series of mysterious fires burned down the warden's house, the social hall, and also the lightkeeper's house. This was significant because the lighthouse was also damaged.

In January 1971, two oil tankers collided in the entrance to the San Francisco Bay. Though everybody acknowledged that the lack of the Alcatraz light wasn't the cause of the collision, this event pushed the federal government to take action. On June 11, 1971, the government had the Coast Guard remove the last fifteen protesters from the island.

Even though the protesters weren't given the title to Alcatraz or even an education center on the island, the occupation was a tremendously meaningful event with lasting impact. It awoke the world to the fact that the US government had broken several hundred treaties with Native Americans, and it helped produce a movement to preserve Native languages and traditions.

On July 8, 1970, President Nixon officially abandoned a 1953 policy designed to strip land, money, and identity from all Native Americans—which likely saved the reservations—and granted Native Americans the right to self-rule.

Here is one section of the Alcatraz Proclamation that reflects living conditions on reservations:

*We feel that this so-called Alcatraz Island is more than suitable for an Indian Reservation, as determined by the white man's own standards. By this we mean that this place resembles most Indian reservations in that:*

1. *It is isolated from modern facilities, and without adequate means of transportation.*
2. *It has no fresh running water.*
3. *It has inadequate sanitation facilities.*
4. *There are no oil or mineral rights.*
5. *There is no industry and so unemployment is very great.*

6. *There are no health care facilities.*

7. *The soil is rocky and non-productive; and the land does not support game.*

8. *There are no educational facilities.*

9. *The population has always exceeded the land base.*

10. *The population has always been held as prisoners and kept dependent upon others.*

*Further, it would be fitting and symbolic that ships from all over the world, entering the Golden Gate, would first see Indian land, and thus be reminded of the true history of this nation. This tiny island would be a symbol of the great lands once ruled by free and noble Indians.*

Alcatraz Occupation 1969

## YOU CAN STILL SEE IT TODAY

When you arrive at the dock, you will see political writings left behind from the Native American occupation. They added the words "Indians Welcome" to the United States Property sign on Building 64.

At the time, they also changed "United States Property" to "United Indian Property." Today the sign has been restored to the 1934 wording: United States Penitentiary.

The sign above the administration building in the cell house at the upper terrace has been altered so that the red and white stripes on the shield below the eagle spell the word *FREE*.

# CHAPTER 17
# WHY WERE SO MANY BUILDINGS ON ALCATRAZ DESTROYED?

After the end of the Native American occupation, the US government feared Alcatraz would attract other activists. Some buildings were destroyed by suspicious fires set at the end of the occupation. The General Services Administration, a government agency that manages federal property, thought about bulldozing all the remaining buildings on Alcatraz to prevent more occupations. They started with the living quarters on the parade grounds. But all the other buildings remained intact because somebody realized there was historical value in what remained.

In 1972, the Golden Gate National Recreation Area was formed, and Alcatraz became a part of it. The initial idea was they would open the island up for tours for only five years. Many people wanted to see Alcatraz for themselves, and it has remained popular since the first tour to the public on October 26, 1973. In the beginning, there were ranger-led tours across the island. Then, in the 1980s, it became an audio tour. Today the voices of four former inmates and four former guards will lead you through the walls of Alcatraz.

## YOU CAN STILL SEE IT TODAY

The bulldozed apartment building left a large rubble pile near the parade grounds that now serves as a nesting site for seagulls. The parade grounds close for several months every year to allow birds to nest safely away from tourists and raise their young. More than a thousand pairs of Western gulls nest on the island every year, with the same partner in nearly the same exact spot. Alcatraz is one of the largest nesting sites for Western gulls on the West Coast.

# CHAPTER 18
# DO PEOPLE REALLY SWIM FROM ALCATRAZ TO SAN FRANCISCO?

Yes. All the time. People have always swum in the San Francisco Bay. And swimming to Alcatraz—or around Alcatraz—has been going on for a long time. When it was first announced in 1934 that Alcatraz was going to be turned into a federal penitentiary, a teenage girl swam from Alcatraz to the shore in forty-seven minutes in protest and to demonstrate how escapable the place would be. In 2016, a nine-year-old boy swam the mile and a half to Alcatraz and the mile and a half back easily. There are large groups that swim with Coast Guard approval multiple times a year. Some groups start at the St. Francis Yacht Club in San Francisco and swim out to circle the island before returning to shore.

The currents are strong, and the water is cold. John Cantwell, the former National Park Service ranger who oversaw Alcatraz for over thirty years, says his hands got so cold he started to lose feeling, and they became like claws. Wetsuits aren't required, but about 90 percent of bay swimmers do wear them.

It would have been a tough swim for any inmates who attempted an escape at night. The water is dark, cold, and choppy. There's a flood tide where water flows into the bay, and an ebb tide where water flows out to the ocean, and a slack tide where the water doesn't move much at all. A typical day, it will flow twice, ebb twice, and be slack four times. Most escape attempts occurred during an ebb tide, and those men were probably taken out to sea. The currents are strongest near the narrowest point of the bay, which is called the Golden Gate. Also, there are sharks.

Do man-eating sharks dwell in the waters around Alcatraz? Yes. On October 10, 2015, while docked at the wharf, the Alcatraz Cruises ferry captured on camera a great white shark breeching out of the water and eating either a sea lion or a seal. Not much of the animal is visible in the footage, and the water quickly fills with bright red blood.

While there's never been a recorded great white shark attack in the bay, tracking shows that they are there. A boy and his dog were attacked by a sevengill shark in 1926 near Alameda. There was one fatal great white shark encounter outside the bay at Baker Beach in 1959: An eighteen-year-old, Albert Kogler, got severely injured by a shark in neck-deep water at dusk. His girlfriend, Shirley O'Neill, stayed beside him during the attack. It took her twenty minutes to get Albert back to shore. President John F. Kennedy awarded Shirley the Young American Medal for Bravery for her actions.

Considering the millions of hours people spend in this water, it's clear that the waters are safer for people than they are for sharks, which are still fished recreationally. Although you might encounter an aggressive sea lion now and then, swimmers say the most hazardous part of the bay is shipping traffic (large container ships and tankers for business shipping).

## YOU CAN STILL SEE IT TODAY

Between late September and February 1, you'll be able to walk the Agave Trail. This path is only open when birds aren't nesting. From this trail you can stand at water level and see the path the swimmers take to the mainland when starting out near Alcatraz Island. If you really research and time your visit, you can stand at the docks in San Francisco and watch them swim ashore.

# CHAPTER 19
# DID PRISONERS EVER RETURN TO ALCATRAZ AS TOURISTS?

Yes. Going as far back as the mid-1980s, there have been annual alumni gatherings on the island, among former correctional officers, convicts, and families that lived on the island when it was an operating prison. People are usually shocked to learn that a federal penitentiary had an alumni program. The convicts and the officers would give talks throughout the island and answer questions from visitors. During Robert Luke's first time back on the island, he was actually nervous about how people would treat him. He worried visitors would judge him for his past crimes. Instead, people treated him like a rock star, mobbing him to ask questions, get photos, and even an autograph. Former officer Bill Long, who found the fake head on the morning after the 1962 escape, still seemed upset that whoever was the guard before him didn't do a standing head count when they heard noise of the roof.

In addition to the alumni gatherings, one former inmate visited Alcatraz and took a tour while he was on the run from the FBI! James "Whitey" Bulger, an inmate from 1959 to 1963, was a wanted man when he visited the island in the mid-1990s as a tourist with his girlfriend, Catherine. The couple took a souvenir photo showing each standing behind mock bars wearing matching prison-striped costumes, while Whitey held a prop ball and chain. It would be another decade before he was apprehended in 2011 by the FBI in Santa Monica, California, after a sixteen-year manhunt.

One former Alcatraz inmate, Frank Hatfield, returned not as a tourist but as a park ranger. Upon his release from prison, Frank became a very popular ranger on Alcatraz, offering tourists dramatic stories of the six years he spent behind bars on The Rock.

## YOU CAN STILL SEE IT TODAY

Although most of the Alcatraz prisoners have died, you can still read about them. Quite a few former inmates wrote memoirs: Leon "Whitey" Thompson, Nathan Glenn Williams, Darwin E. Coon, George Pitts, Robert Luke, John Dekker, John Banner, Roy Gardner, William G. Baker, and Jim Quillen. You can find many of their books in the cell house bookstore.

BOOKSTORE

# CHAPTER 20
# COULD ALCATRAZ EVER BE A PRISON AGAIN?

No. Not only is Alcatraz too expensive to maintain as a prison, but it would be far too expensive to update. When it first shut down, people had all sorts of ideas for what Alcatraz could become—an amusement park, a nudist colony, a peace monument, a casino—but it's surviving just fine the way it is: as a tourist destination for anyone who is curious about where America used to hold its most dangerous criminals.

One of the biggest obstacles Alcatraz faced—and continues to face—in being used as a fort or a military prison is its lack of a natural source of water. Even when Alcatraz operated, the toilets flushed with seawater, and everything drained into the bay. Today the water tower on the island isn't functional, and water still must be barged onto the island. Wastewater has to be removed.

Seabirds, who don't need fresh water and can excrete salt water through salt glands and ducts connected to their bills, seem to be the only perfect occupants for the island. Year after year, their numbers grow: Western gulls, California gulls, snowy egrets, black-crowned night herons, Brandt's cormorants, Pelagic cormorants, double-crested cormorants, pigeon guillemots, black oystercatchers, and a pair of peregrine falcons. With so much of the island off-limits to people, it feels as if the island has come full circle from where its story began and has returned to the birds.

## YOU CAN STILL SEE IT TODAY

If you like birds, come in the summer. You will see them, and their poop, everywhere. The snowy egrets nest in the fig trees on the island's west side, below the cell house, close to the island's edge. You can see them from the main road.

If you like flies, come in August.

# CONCLUSION

**W**hen I was a volunteer gardener on the island, I thought a lot about the prisoners. What did it feel like to arrive there? What did it feel like to leave? One convict who died very near where I gardened is somebody I still think about. Here's his story:

There's only one road on Alcatraz, the main road. Gardening on the island, week after week, I followed the same path around the island every visit. Like most tourist sites, Alcatraz has signs placed in certain areas to provide historical information to visitors. I probably passed them thirty times before I finally stopped to read them. One, on the west side, right next to the cliffs and the old prison gate, is a sign memorializing the first escape attempt from Alcatraz. There are almost no details about Joseph Bowers other than his name and a brief description explaining why he was shot to death beside this spot on April 27, 1936.

Joseph Bowers was the first federal prisoner to try to escape from Alcatraz, while working at his job at the incinerator. How Joseph ended up working at that incinerator is a sad story. He was born to circus performers in El Paso, Texas, who abandoned him at birth. He never went to school and was raised by other circus workers. Joseph ended up in federal prison because he robbed a store that had a post office inside it. For a theft of approximately sixteen dollars, Joseph was given a twenty-five-year prison sentence. He didn't fit in well at Alcatraz and was put into solitary confinement. Then he was given the terrible job of getting rid of all the garbage from Alcatraz. Over and over, he hauled trash to the oven. Burned it. Scraped the ashes down a chute into the water. He used to find leftover food in the kitchen waste and feed the seagulls. On the day of his escape, he stacked trashcans to reach the top of the fence. A guard noticed him on top of the fence. Joseph didn't respond to warnings to climb down. The guard fired. And fired again. And again.

Joseph fell onto the rocks. Prison officials could only reach his wounded body by boat. By the time they got him to the hospital, Joseph had already died.

Should Joseph have been sent to Alcatraz for his minor crime? Were the strict rules on Alcatraz, including the silence policy, a good idea? Not long after Joseph's death, Warden Johnston ended the silence policy, one of the only rule changes ever made in the prison. The island sits in the bay, its blocky, gray prison immediately recognizable. It holds countless stories. If you visit Alcatraz Island, there are many things you can still see today, but there are also many that will always remain a mystery.

# BIBLIOGRAPHY

Babyak, Jolene. *Breaking the Rock: The Great Escape from Alcatraz*. Berkeley, CA: Ariel Vamp Press, 2001.

Beatty, Russell A. "Lessons from the Gardens of Alcatraz." *Pacific Horticulture Magazine*, 1997

Bergreen, Laurence. *Capone: The Man and the Era*. New York: Touchstone, 1994.

Blansett, Kent. *A Journey to Freedom: Richard Oakes, Alcatraz, and the Red Power Movement*. New Haven, CT: Yale University Press, 2018.

Bruce, J. Campbell. *Escape from Alcatraz*. Berkeley, CA: Ten Speed Press, 2005.

Butler, Rick, dir. *Lonely Island: Hidden Alcatraz*. A KQED Production, 2002.

DeVincenzi, George. *Murders on Alcatraz*. The Rock, 2014.

Delgado, James P. *Alcatraz: The Story Behind the Scenery*. Las Vegas, NV: K. C. Publications, 1985.

Eig, Jonathon. *Get Capone: The Secret Plot That Captured America's Most Wanted Gangster*. New York: Simon & Schuster, 2011.

*Escapes from Alcatraz: The True Stories*. Michael Hoff Productions, 2010.

Esslinger, Michael. *Alcatraz: A Definitive History of the Penitentiary Years*. San Francisco, CA: Ocean View Publishing, 2006.

Forsling, Jon. *Alcatraz: The Last Survivors*. Create Space, 2018.

Fortier, James M., dir. *Alcatraz Is Not an Island*. Diamond Island Productions, 2001.

Gardner, Roy. *Hellcatraz: The Rock of Despair*. Self-published, 1938.

Hart, John, Russell A. Beatty, Michael Boland, and Roy Eisenhardt. *Gardens of Alcatraz*. San Francisco, CA: Golden Gate National Parks Association, 1996.

Johnson, Mayme, and Karen E. Quinones Miller. *Harlem Godfather: The Rap on My Husband, Ellsworth "Bumpy" Johnson*. Philadelphia, PA: Oshum Publishing Company, 2008.

Johnston, James A. *Alcatraz Island Prison and the Men Who Live There*. New York: Charles Scribner's Sons, 1949.

Karpis, Alvin. *On the Rock: Twenty-Five Years in Alcatraz*. Don Mills, Ontario: Musson Book Company, 1980.

Lageson, Ernest B. *Battle at Alcatraz: A Desperate Attempt to Escape the Rock*. Omaha, NE: Addicus Books, Inc., 1999.

Martini, John A. *Fortress Alcatraz: Guardian of the Golden Gate*. Kailua, HI: Pacific Monograph, 1991.

Quillen, Jim. *Alcatraz from Inside: The Hard Years, 1942–1952*. San Francisco, CA: Golden Gate National Park Association, 1991.

Schoenberg, Robert J. *Mr. Capone*. New York: Quill, 1992.

*Secrets of Alcatraz*. Golden Gate National Parks Conservancy, 1992.

Smith, Paul Chaat, and Robert Allen Warrior. *Like a Hurricane: The Indian Movement from Alcatraz to Wounded Knee*. New York: The New Press, 1996.

Thompson, Erwin N. *The Rock: A History of Alcatraz Island, 1947–1972*. Historic Preservation Division, National Park Service, United Sates Department of the Interior, 1979.

Ward, David A., and Gene G. Kassebaum. *Alcatraz: The Gangster Years*. Berkeley, CA: University of California Press, 2009.

# ACKNOWLEDGMENTS

This book wouldn't exist if it weren't for the many interviews people agreed to have with me by phone and email. Ranger John Cantwell spent over a year generously sharing stories and recommending books. If not for him, there would be no book. For fielding all my history questions, and always having an answer, I'd like to thank John Martini. For discussing the making of the world-famous Alcatraz audio tour, I'm grateful to Nicki Phelps, Chris Tellis, and Chris Hardman. For generously providing me with correspondence with Elliott Michener and answering all my garden questions, I'm very grateful to Russell Beatty, who passed away during the final edits of this book. I'm deeply appreciative to David Ward, who wrote the most astonishingly thorough book about Alcatraz and reopened his notes to answer my questions. David McGuire, founder and director of the shark and marine conservation nonprofit "Shark Stewards," gave incredibly helpful information regarding sharks in San Francisco Bay, and I'm grateful for his help. I'm also grateful to James P. Delgado and Adrian Burton for their thoughtful responses to my queries concerning seabirds and Alcatraz. I'm also thankful to archivist Sean Heyliger, who pulled all the materials I needed and offered expert advice multiple times during my research at the National Archives in San Bruno. NARA archivists Aaron Seltzer and Charles Miller also assisted me in this research.

I'm extremely grateful to Amanda Williford, supervisory curator for the Golden Gate National Recreation Area's Park Archives in the Presidio, who helped me locate historical Alcatraz photographs and letters and also oral histories. So many Alcatraz gardeners shared stories with me over many years, and I'm thankful for the many ways they contributed to this book, especially Dick Miner, Corny Foster, Marney Beard, Monica Beary, Barbara Howald, Tracy Roberts, and Kristin Scheel. Of course this journey wouldn't have been possible without my friend Shelagh Fritz, who signed me up to volunteer in the gardens many, many years ago. The greatest gift to shaping this book is Paula Manzanero, whose thoughtful and generous editing made this book far more polished, compact, and focused than I dreamed it could be—THANK YOU! And many thanks for the masterful copyedits provided by Rebecca Behrens. And my agent, Sara Crowe, deserves so much thanks for always supporting my books and ideas and also for finding the book's fabulous illustrator, Anika Orrock. Last, never least, thanks to my husband, Brian, and son, Max. It's through sharing Alcatraz with them that I found this book. Nothing would mean anything without them.